ARCHBISHOP RIORDAN HIGH SCHOOL

T 12829

P9-BBV-913

DATE DUE

5/21			
12/16			
5/25			
5/24			
GAYLORD			PRINTED IN U.S.A.

THE END OF AFFIRMATIVE ACTION

ALSO BY DARIEN A. MCWHIRTER

Your Rights at Work
Sharing Ownership
Privacy in the Workplace (with Jon Bible)
Privacy as a Constitutional Right (with Jon Bible)
The Personnel Policy Handbook for Growing Companies
Managing People: Creating the Team-Based Organization
The Separation of Church and State
Freedom of Speech, Press, and Assembly
Search, Seizure, and Privacy
Equal Protection

THE END OF AFFIRMATIVE ACTION

WHERE DO WE GO FROM HERE?

DARIEN A. McWHIRTER

A BIRCH LANE PRESS BOOK
Published by Carol Publishing Group

98 182

Copyright © 1996 by Darien A. McWhirter
All rights reserved. No part of this book may be reproduced in any form, except by a newspaper or magazine reviewer who wishes to quote brief passages in connnection with a review.

A Birch Lane Press Book
Published by Carol Publishing Group
Birch Lane Press is a registered trademark of Carol Communications, Inc.
Editorial Offices: 600 Madison Avenue, New York, N.Y. 10022
Sales and Distribution Offices: 120 Enterprise Avenue, Secaucus, N.J. 07094
In Canada: Canadian Manda Group, One Atlantic Avenue, Suite 105, Toronto,
   Ontario M6K 3E7
Queries regarding rights and permissions should be addressed to Carol
Publishing Group, 600 Madison Avenue, New York, N.Y. 10022

Carol Publishing Group books are available at special discounts for bulk purchases, sales promotion, fund-raising, or educational purposes. Special editions can be created to specifications. For details, contact: Special Sales Department, Carol Publishing Group, 120 Enterprise Avenue, Secaucus, N.J. 07094

Manufactured in the United States of America
10 9 8 7 6 5 4 3 2 1

Library of Congress Cataloging-in-Publication Data

McWhirter, Darien A. (Darien Auburn)
   The end of affirmative action: where do we go from here? / Darien A.
   McWhirter.
      p.   cm.
   "A Birch Lane Press book."
   ISBN 1-55972-339-4 (hardcover)
   1. Affirmative action programs—United States.   2. Discrimination in
employment—United States.   3. Reverse discrimination in employment—
United States.   4. Affirmative action programs—Law and legislation—
United States.   I. Title.
HF5549.5.A34M38   1996
331.13′3′0973—dc20   95-50095
                                                                  CIP

To my mother

CONTENTS

ACKNOWLEDGMENTS

I want to express my deep appreciation to Carol Justus for all her help and encouragement. I want to thank Nils Pearson for his help with research and Dorene Cohen for her advice on the manuscript. I would also like to thank John Engell for his advice and encouragement.

I could never have completed this book without the aid of my longtime friend Bernice Borak. Her perspective on the topic, as seen from outside the country, was invaluable. Her comments on the manuscript were very helpful.

I want to thank my copy editor, Frank Lavena, my production editor, Carrie Cantor, and production manager, Donald Davidson, for their help in bringing this project to press.

Last, but not least, I want to thank my editor, Jim Ellison, for his willingness to read this manuscript not once, but twice, and make hundreds of helpful comments on both occasions.

While I have been as diligent as possible, errors are inevitable in any project of this type. I apologize for them. I have worked to make sure every statement of history and law is as accurate as possible.

INTRODUCTION

On October 17, 1995, as almost a million black men marched on Washington, D.C., President Bill Clinton spoke about race relations at the University of Texas at Austin. He pointed out that in the wake of the O. J. Simpson verdict no one could deny that "white Americans and black Americans often see the same world in drastically different ways." He suggested that whites "must understand and acknowledge the roots of black pain" and that blacks "must understand and acknowledge the roots of white fear." As for affirmative action, he said that we must "mend it, not end it." But what does that mean? How exactly will we mend it? He presented no specifics.

This presidential speech continued a discussion that began early in 1995, when several of the Republican candidates for president vowed to "end" affirmative action if they were elected. What would they end exactly, and why? What would that mean to real people in their everyday world? It seemed that when it came to affirmative action, everyone assumed that if America really debated the issue, it would lead to division and conflict, not understanding and answers, so no real debate was forthcoming.

In April and May 1995, PBS's *MacNeil/Lehrer News Hour* asked one of its correspondents, Charlayne Hunter-Gault, a black woman, to conduct a series of interviews concerning affirmative action. She began the series on April 17 by interviewing Ruth Simmons, the provost of Princeton University. Ruth Simmons, who is black, said that the perception by some white males that women and minorities had somehow been given an unfair advantage because of affirmative action was untrue. She felt that the debate about affirmative action had been dishonest because of this emphasis on what she called "affirmative preference."

During this first interview, Hunter-Gault asked if thirty years of affirmative action was long enough to make up for centuries of discrimination against black people; Ruth Simmons said that thirty years was certainly not long enough. When Hunter-Gault asked how we would know when it was time to end affirmative action, Simmons suggested that we could conduct a survey and ask white men if they were willing to change their sex and race. If a large percentage of them said yes, then perhaps it would be time to end affirmative action.

Hunter-Gault then asked Simmons about the argument that affirmative action stigmatizes minorities and women because it suggests that they cannot compete on an equal basis with white men. Simmons did not think that affirmative action led to stigmatization of anyone. When asked about the argument that affirmative action meant lower standards, Simmons pointed out that universities have always had lower standards when it came to admitting athletes and the children of wealthy alumni. Then Hunter-Gault asked if it might not be time to get back to the original intent of the civil rights laws, the idea of color-blind and gender-blind decisions. Simmons raised the problem of poor kids in the ghettos and asked what would become of them without affirmative action.

In the course of the series, Hunter-Gault interviewed two other strong supporters of affirmative action: David Lawrence, the publisher of the *Miami Herald*, and Herma Hill Kaye, the dean of the University of California at Berkeley School of Law.

David Lawrence quickly acknowledged that the newsrooms of America had not done a very good job of achieving racial integration and said that affirmative action should continue for "as long as it takes." Lawrence felt that the general public was uninformed about the issue. He did not believe affirmative action was about "quotas or lower standards," but he did not make it clear exactly what he thought affirmative action *was* about.

Herma Hill Kaye pointed out that when she entered the University of California at Berkeley School of Law in 1960, there were no minorities and very few women among the student body. By the 1990s there was no longer an affirmative-action program for women because it was no longer needed. Women could meet the usual criteria for admission without special quotas or lower standards. Minorities still received special treatment through the affirmative-action program, and she felt that it should continue. Hill Kaye felt that it was not yet time for America to end affirmative-action programs that give preferences based on sex and race.

Hunter-Gault asked her about the fact that the major justification for affirmative action had been the suffering of African Americans and yet the major beneficiary of affirmative action had been white women like herself. Hill Kaye could only respond by saying that white women had suffered, too. Hunter-Gault then asked if a public debate about affirmative action would be helpful. Hill Kaye expressed concern that an open debate might exacerbate racial tension. When asked if programs based on poverty could replace programs based on race and sex, Hill Kaye answered with an emphatic no. In her mind, the only way to help minorities and women was with affirmative-action programs that targeted minorities and women.

Ruth Simmons, David Lawrence, and Herma Hill Kaye expressed the classic liberal line on affirmative action. It is apparently a position that President Clinton and others have decided to take and one that I certainly agreed with during the 1970s and into the 1980s. How could we expect people who had suffered decades of discrimination to catch up overnight simply because the heavy hand of discrimination had been lifted? Surely something more was needed, and that was clearly some form of affirmative action. At the same time, during the 1980s, I wondered why, if affirmative action makes so much sense, America couldn't discuss it openly. Why couldn't Congress pass laws and set up procedures to clarify how and when affirmative action was to be used?

The three liberal supporters of affirmative action Charlayne Hunter-Gault interviewed did not have ready answers to many important questions. Everyone assumes that affirmative action is a temporary program. How will we know when to end it? Can we end it for this group and not for that group? Can we end it here and not there? What about the argument that although the main justification for affirmative action is the need to help Americans who are both poor and black, most of those who have benefited from it are neither poor nor black? I had wondered at the end of the 1980s, and again when watching these interviews, if it was not time to question a policy that a majority of Americans, according to opinion surveys conducted over three decades, have always objected to and that even its strongest supporters could not elucidate.

To balance these three supporters of affirmative action, Hunter-Gault interviewed four critics of affirmative action, two white and two black. The two white critics were John Silber, the president of Boston University, and Abigail Thernstrom, a political scientist and a senior fellow at the Manhattan Institute, a conservative think tank in New York City.

Silber began by pointing out the difficulty everyone seems to have defining what affirmative action is. He said that it was the original intent of the civil rights laws to remove criteria such as sex and race from the decision-making process when it comes to deciding who gets a job or a university education. He felt that merit should be the key and that discrimination in favor of the members of this or that group was a mistake. He pointed out that his university had denied tenure to an unqualified female faculty member and had been sued as a result. The university had won the case, but only after paying $450,000 in legal fees. Silber suggested that many universities granted tenure to unqualified women and minority faculty rather than face lawsuits and potentially large attorney's bills.

He argued that we should get rid of affirmative-action programs because they fail to really address the problems of the black underclass. He felt that for black people living in the urban ghettos, many of whom do not graduate from high school, affirmative action as applied to college admissions and employment never touches their lives.

Abigail Thernstrom stated her position quickly: She had always been against racial sorting and double standards. On the other hand, she had never opposed the use of affirmative action to remedy specific cases of proven discrimination. She felt that the use of double standards to make admission decisions at universities was clearly wrong. At the same time, she believed that expanding the criteria used to make college admission decisions would have a more positive impact on minorities than current affirmative-action programs. Thernstrom was particularly troubled by the fact that in many organizations the people in charge were not willing to "fess up" to exactly what they were doing. Too often, in her experience, those who engaged in affirmative action argued that this was not what they were really doing. She suggested that it was time for everyone to put his cards on the table.

In Thernstrom's mind there is only one long-term solution to the problems faced by minorities in America, and that is to make major improvements in the education they receive. She also argued that the only way to achieve real equality is to treat people as individuals, not as representatives of their race or sex. When asked how we could make up for centuries of discrimination against African Americans, she answered that it was not possible to do so; furthermore, any attempt to try was doomed to failure. She ended the interview by saying that this subject had been allowed to fester far too long and that she hoped an open debate would help to clear the air. She felt that the real question is: What do we, as a society, really believe in?

Hunter-Gault also interviewed two black men who had openly criticized affirmative action: Ward Connerly, a businessman and a member of the University of California Board of Regents, and Shelby Steele, a professor of English at San Jose State University and author of *The Content of Our Character*.

Connerly began by pointing out that affirmative action encompasses many programs and that some of them should continue. He made a distinction between affirmative recruitment (working to encourage minorities to apply for college and jobs), on the one hand, and affirmative preference (giving minorities an absolute preference in admissions and hiring), on the other. He felt that the time for affirmative preference was over. When Hunter-Gault asked about the centuries of discrimination suffered by black people, Connerly pointed out that affirmative preference is not just reserved for black people. Many white women and other minorities have received the benefits of affirmative preference. He felt that affirmative-preference programs had harmed people and that in California in particular both whites and Asians had been denied opportunities because of affirmative-preference programs. He also took the position that affirmative action creates a stigma, particularly for African Americans. In other words, by the 1990s, in his opinion, affirmative action had helped a lot of people other than blacks, and blacks had suffered stigmatization as a result. In his view, African Americans were being blamed for a program that seldom benefited them.

Connerly did suggest, however, that affirmative recruitment should continue. He also pointed out that American society was not giving many African-American children the kind of education from kindergarten through twelfth grade that they needed to advance in the society. He saw this as the major problem for black people in the 1990s. At the same time, he felt that setting aside a percentage of government contracts for women and minority-owned firms did not really accomplish much and that the practice should end.

When Hunter-Gault asked Connerly about President Clinton's response to the issue, he expressed disappointment. Clinton had just visited California and spoken to a group of Democratic party leaders. The president suggested that something had to be done to placate angry white men. According to Connerly, surveys in California showed that two-thirds of the voting-age population thought it was time to end affirmative-preference programs. Since white men made up less than one-third of the people surveyed, there was clearly something more going on than just the anger of white men.

In Connerly's judgment, President Lyndon Johnson's major contribution to affirmative action was the creation of the Head Start program in the 1960s. He suggested that it was time to get back to the idea of preparing people to enter the race through educational programs rather than trying to make up for a lack of preparation with quotas and lower standards.

The final interview, held on May 4, was with black author Shelby Steele, who began by saying he did not think programs that give people a preference because of their race or gender should continue. On the other hand, he believed that affirmative-recruitment programs should continue. He believed that affirmative action was an attempt by society to avoid serious social development and educational reform for poor people, particularly poor minorities. In his opinion, affirmative action was cheap compared to what it would cost to make a meaningful difference in the lives of poor blacks living in urban America. As an example, he pointed out that 75 percent of the black students who enter San Jose State University drop out. Thus, in his mind, the whole idea of affirmative preference was a swindle. In his experience, the main beneficiaries of affirmative action had been middle- and upper-class white women, not poor minorities. He felt that affirmative action was designed to assist the poor but actually helped, primarily, the nonpoor. While President Johnson's Great Society programs had tried to address some of the nation's problems, affirmative action had turned out to be a patronage program for middle-class white women.

Steele then said that he could not conceive of a worse program for middle-class blacks than affirmative preference. It stigmatized them and suggested that they could not really live up to the standard. In his opinion, more blacks would have gotten ahead faster if there had never been any affirmative-action programs that granted preferences on the basis of race. He felt that all the energy of the civil rights movement had been "bought off" with affirmative action and that more would be accomplished if African Americans demanded equal expenditures for the education of black children instead of affirmative-preference programs.

He also made the point that white males had a right to be angry because they had been disadvantaged and that affirmative action had amounted to institutionally sanctioned discrimination based on race and sex. In Steele's opinion, America needs to move away from affirmative preference. He also said that the debate about affirmative action was the best thing that had happened since the civil rights movement of the 1960s. He hoped Americans would be forced to examine it as a social policy and actually communicate with each other.

These seven people voiced almost all the views that have been expressed about affirmative action in recent years. While some said that affirmative action had meant hiring unqualified people and using quotas, others believed that it had not. While some felt that affirmative action had been bad for minorities because it stigmatized them, others suggested that affirmative action had not stigmatized anyone. While some felt that affirmative action mainly helped middle-class white women, others believed that poor minorities would be lost without it.

At the same time, there were clearly some issues they all could agree on. All seven seemed to agree that affirmative recruitment is a good idea. They were unanimous in their view that America does not do enough to help poor children receive the kind of education below the college level that would help them achieve success in college and later in life. Many of them felt that at least some of the benefits of affirmative preference had gone to people who did not deserve a special preference at the expense of people who did not deserve to be victimized.

I found myself most in agreement with Ward Connerly and Shelby Steele. I lived in California from 1989 to 1994 and was appalled by the misuse of affirmative action. It was seldom used to help poor black people get ahead. In my field of vision, it was used mainly by white women to help promote their personal friends outside the "usual" process. Often the "victims" of this biased system were women or minorities who would have gotten the job or the promotion if the usual criteria had been used. In a sense, all women and minorities were stigmatized by a system that presumed that they could not compete on an equal basis when in fact they were perfectly capable of doing so.

I decided to write this book because I was unable to find one that presented the basic information about law and policy that anyone who wants to discuss this issue intelligently should have. At the same time, I certainly do have a point of view. It is that of the disillusioned liberal who has seen a progressive idea twisted and abused to the point where it now appears to do more harm than good to those it was designed to help in the first place. It appears that America during the second half of the 1990s is destined to examine many of the programs put in place over the course of half a century. I do not think that is in itself a bad idea. We must remember why such programs were initiated and be willing to change them if they no longer serve the purpose for which they were created. Some aspects of affirmative action, in my opinion, now fall into that category.

I would also like to point out that while I began this book in an effort to explain why I, as a liberal, had decided it was time to end some aspects of affirmative action, a funny thing happened on the way to its completion. The Supreme Court ruled on June 12, 1995, that most racial preference programs are now unconstitutional. For reasons that are not clear, both the media and politicians such as President Clinton have chosen to ignore the clear implications of that decision. One of the goals of this book is to help everyone understand what its implications are. Just as it no longer made sense to talk about keeping public schools segregated by race after the Supreme Court's *Brown* decision in 1954, it no longer makes sense to talk about maintaining most racial-preference programs after the Supreme Court's *Adarand* decision in 1995.

Affirmative action has been billed as one of the most divisive issues of the last quarter of the twentieth century. I believe that some of that devisiveness is an illusion. While there is certainly a difference of opinion about affirmative action, opinion polls show that a majority of whites, women, and minorities have been against race- and gender-based preference programs throughout this period. At the same time, a majority of public officials have been in favor of them. In a very real sense, the division has been between what public officials felt the society needed and what people actually wanted, not between whites and minorities or men and women. The media have only contributed to this confusion by failing to present in any detail what was really going on. I hope that this book will help end some of that confusion.

THE END OF AFFIRMATIVE ACTION

1

COMING TO TERMS
WITH TERMS

Affirmative Action: two words that conjure up a wide variety of meanings, depending on who is speaking and who is listening. It is a term that has had many definitions and has provoked very intense feelings. Some equate affirmative action with the whole civil rights movement and see an attack on any aspect of it as an assault on the legacy of such civil rights leaders as Martin Luther King Jr. Others feel that affirmative action is nothing short of a betrayal of everything those leaders fought so hard to achieve.

Affirmative action has legal, political, and social dimensions. As a legal concept it occupies a strange place in the legal lexicon. You would look in vain for a definition of affirmative action in the statutes of the federal government or the decisions of the U.S. Supreme Court. The feeling seems to have been that the concept, if we defined it, would lose some of its magical qualities. Politicians have used it in the most cynical ways imaginable to achieve reelection, allowing the context of their statements to convey the appropriate message. Social scientists have generally avoided it, which makes affirmative action unique in the world of American social policy. No other important policy of the twentieth century has had such an impact on people's lives and so little social-scientific investigation of its real impact—either on society in general or on individuals and groups in particular.

Surveys appear to prove that the American people are strangely confused about this issue. However, much of the apparent

3

confusion has more to do with the way survey questions are worded than with what the average person actually thinks. In the spring of 1995 a *Washington Post*–ABC poll of 1,524 randomly selected Americans showed that three out of four opposed affirmative action programs that "give preference to minorities or women to make up for past discrimination." Almost half, 47 percent, said they wanted the programs changed; 28 percent favored their elimination entirely. Only 23 percent said they should be left as they are. At the same time, a Gallup poll showed that 55 percent of Americans favored affirmative action. Why the difference?

Actually, there is no difference in opinion, just in wording. When one 1995 poll asked: "Do you think that blacks and other minorities should receive preference in hiring, promotions, and college admissions to make up for past discrimination?" 24 percent said yes, and 75 percent said no, with 46 percent of blacks and 81 percent of whites saying no. On the other hand, in response to the general question "All in all, do you favor or oppose affirmative-action programs for blacks and other minority groups?" 46 percent said "favor" and 41 percent said "oppose." The same people who favored affirmative action in general were then asked more detailed questions, and a clearer picture emerged.

When asked about the use of hiring goals for women and minorities, 59 percent were opposed; when asked about having college scholarship programs only for black or minority students, 78 percent were opposed; and when asked about set-aside programs to guarantee that a percentage of government contracts will be awarded to minority-owned firms, 59 percent were opposed.[1]

In other words, polls suggest that Americans are in favor of some aspects of what generally goes by the name of affirmative action and are opposed to others. The key to understanding the issue becomes one of definition.

DEFINING AFFIRMATIVE ACTION

Affirmative action is at least three things. First, there is affirmative recruitment. Affirmative recruitment means that a school or employer aggressively encourages minorities or women to apply for a job or a place in the entering class. A college might send students or professors into an inner-city neighborhood to help high school students understand what college is all about and gain the confidence needed to apply. An employer might advertise job openings in newspapers that have a large minority readership. While often lost in the heated debate about affirmative action, affirmative recruitment has been an important part of America's effort to bring more minorities into the mainstream of work and education. When we think of the military's efforts to achieve a more integrated force, we think first of the significant amount of time and money that has been spent encouraging minorities to view the military as a way up and out of poverty. Affirmative recruitment has helped turn one of the most racially divided organizations in society into one of the most racially integrated. Colin Powell, as the nation's top soldier, stands as a symbol of that achievement. Most Americans seem to favor affirmative recruitment.

A second meaning of the term affirmative action is *affirmative fairness*. Affirmative fairness means going out of the way to make sure a woman or minority candidate for a college entering class, a job, or a promotion has been treated fairly. In the college context, fair treatment may mean looking at the particular background of a student to ascertain if it is fair to apply the usual admission requirements in his or her particular case. Has a student lived in circumstances that make it unlikely that the standard admission test will really measure his or her mental ability? Has the student had to overcome obstacles to finish high school that other students did not face? Do the usual measures applied to suburban middle-class students really tell us much about the student? In the job context the question is: Has a particular candidate really been judged on merit, or have sexism or racism been a factor in the evaluation process? Most Americans seem to favor affirmative fairness.

The third idea many people have in mind when they use the term affirmative action is *affirmative preference*. By affirmative preference we mean that if someone is the "right" sex or the "right" race they are preferred over someone who is the "wrong" sex or race. This preference can seem minor, such as preferring someone of a particular race or sex when both candidates are essentially equal. The preference can seem more significant, however, when a highly qualified candidate for college admission or a job or a promotion is passed over for a woman or minority applicant who is clearly less qualified. Because social scientists have not had the courage to study the phenomenon, we do not know how often this has happened since 1970, when affirmative action became a significant part of the American landscape. Critics say it occurs all the time and is destroying America. Supporters say it almost never happens. The truth, we have to suspect, lies somewhere in between.

THE JUSTIFICATION

Often lost in discussions of affirmative action are the reasons why America, as a society, decided to implement it. During the course of the last three decades of the twentieth century, three reasons emerged to justify affirmative action.

The first, and in the minds of many the most legitimate, justification for engaging in affirmative preference is the need to compensate for specific instances of race and gender discrimination in the past by particular organizations. When this is the reason for affirmative action, people speak of *specific discrimination*, meaning that a particular union, employer, college, or government agency has engaged in intentional discrimination in the past and only a program of affirmative action will compensate for it. The goal is to reach the level of women and minority students, employees, or contractors that we believe would have been achieved if there had never been any discrimination in the first place. Of course, since race and gender bias was so widespread in society into the 1960s, it is difficult, if not impossible, to really know what that level might have been if women and minorities had never been the victims of intentional discrimination. In southern states, a crude algebra has been used. For example, in Alabama, where a quarter of the high school graduates are black and the main educational requirement for becoming a state police officer is a high school diploma, it is assumed that without past intentional discrimination a quarter of the Alabama state police would be black. To compensate, a federal judge ordered the state of Alabama to make sure that half of its new recruits were black until blacks made up one quarter of the total force. These kinds of calculations become more difficult when we move out of the South and look at jobs that require more in the way of education or other qualifications.

While a few may object to this use of quotas and affirmative preference, most Americans seem to accept the use of affirmative preference to correct instances of specific discrimination. Even Abigail Thernstrom, the most conservative person interviewed by Charlayne Hunter-Gault, accepted the idea of using court-ordered affirmative-preference programs when past discrimination had been proven in a court of law.

The second reason given to justify affirmative action is the need to remedy *societal discrimination*. The college, company, or agency has not engaged in intentional discrimination in the past, but it is clear that other entities in society have. To make up for this past discrimination by others, a particular organization engages in some type of affirmative action. The classic example of this is the college that builds a new medical school and introduces an affirmative-action program for the first entering class. Clearly, there has never been specific discrimination by this medical school, but in order to make up for the discrimination suffered by particular groups in the past at the hands of society in general, the new medical school sets aside a certain number of places in each entering class for minorities.

The third reason given to justify affirmative action is the need to create more *diversity* in a particular organization. In the year 2000 less than one-third of those entering the American work-force will be white and male; the rest will be women and minorities. In other words, America in the twenty-first century will be a very diverse place. How can we expect people to function in such a society if they have lived in neighborhoods and gone to schools only with people who look like them? It is assumed that the more we come to live with, work with, and go to school with people of other genders and races, the better off society will be.

THE SOCIAL CONTEXT

Affirmative action has become such a vague term that it is used in dozens of different contexts to either praise or attack, depending on the speaker and the audience. For the purposes of this discussion, we will limit ourselves to three social contexts: college admissions, job hiring and promotions, and government contracting.

In the context of *college admissions*, the focus from the mid-1970s onward has been on affirmative preference. The stated goal has been to create on each college campus in the United States a microcosm of the race and gender makeup of society at large. The watchword has been diversity. The idea is that people who are going to have to work and live in a very diverse society will be better off if they are exposed to that diversity in college.

In the context of *job hiring and promotions*, the focus has been on every kind of affirmative action, from recruitment to prefer-ence. The most often stated reason for using affirmative action in employment is to make up not only for decades of specific discrimination by companies and government agencies but for discrimination by society in general. Of course, there is a problem. When we ask employers to justify their affirmative-action pro-grams, they open themselves up to liability under the civil rights laws if they admit to past intentional discrimination. Many people have tried to get around this by talking about both specific discrimination and societal discrimination in the same breath, as if they were the same thing.

In the context of *government contracting*, it has been almost impossible to think in terms of compensating for specific acts of discrimination. How could we ever know how many women or minorities might have created companies that might have received government contracts if it had not been for past discrimination? In this context, there is seldom even the pretext of trying to compen-sate for past instances of specific discrimination. Instead, the idea is that society in general has clearly discriminated against some-one, somewhere, and one way to compensate for this is to set aside a certain percentage of government contracts for representatives of the discriminated-against groups.

THE PHILOSOPHICAL CONTEXT

Throughout the debate about affirmative action, looking to the basic philosophical underpinnings of American society has not served to inform the discussion. American society, like all liberal democracies, is based on three basic ideals: democracy, personal freedom, and equality. However, equality means different things to different people in different contexts. Politically, it means that government should treat everyone the same when it comes to voting and running for public office. Economically, it means that everyone should have an equal opportunity to participate to the fullest extent of their abilities. Too often during the last quarter of the twentieth century, the debate over affirmative action has been about the desire to achieve equal opportunity. Both sides of the debate accepted the basic premise that the ultimate goal was equal opportunity. The only question has been how to achieve it in the race for economic success when everyone also agreed that society had engaged in practices that prevented a large number of citizens from even making it to the starting line. One group said that now that these people can get to the starting line, society has done enough for them, and the race should simply be run as fairly as possible from that point forward. The other group said that it does little good to be at the starting line if people don't have the knowledge and experience needed to run the race. Even the staunchest supporters of affirmative action agree that someday affirmative action will not be needed, but it is not clear how we will know when that day has arrived.

THE LEGAL CONTEXT

The legal aspects of the debate have been particularly frustrating for both lawyers and the general public. It may seem strange to realize it today, but when the U.S. Constitution was written, achieving equality was not one of its stated goals. While today we think of equality and democracy as two sides of the same coin, the men who wrote the Constitution did not labor under any such conception. They lived in a society in which most African Americans were slaves, where women could not vote or own property in their own name and men who did not own the minimum amount of real estate could not vote or run for public office. The struggle to add equality to the American concept of democracy and liberty has been the defining challenge of the United States over the first two centuries of its existence.

Equality did not make it into the Constitution until after the Civil War, with the addition of the Fourteenth Amendment. It states simply that no state may "deny to any person within its jurisdiction the equal protection of the laws." It was not until the twentieth century that the Supreme Court had to come to grips with the fact that there is no Equal Protection Clause in the original Constitution and Bill of Rights. Did that mean that states could not discriminate against people based on their race because of the Fourteenth Amendment but the federal government was free to do so? That is exactly what it did mean, and some scholars think we might have been better off if the Supreme Court had simply pointed this out and left it up to society to go through the process of adding an Equal Protection Amendment to the Constitution that applied to the federal government, but the justices did not do that. Instead, they looked to the Fifth Amendment, which states that the federal government must provide everyone with "due process of law" and decided that the concept of "equal protection" was implied in the concept of "due process."

In the course of the twentieth century, when it came to interpreting the idea of equal protection, the Court developed the concepts of "strict scrutiny" and "rationality." For most purposes, the justices said that government was free to treat citizens unequally as long as it had a "rational" reason for doing so. In general, this meant that almost anything government wanted to do was acceptable. The major exception was in the area of race. If a government—state, federal, or local—wanted to single people out because of their race, that kind of discrimination would be subjected to strict scrutiny. To survive strict scrutiny, the action in question would have to be motivated by a "compelling" reason and be "narrowly tailored" to achieve that purpose. When it comes to race discrimination, only two reasons have stood up to strict scrutiny since 1944. The Supreme Court has allowed race discrimination to protect the nation in time of war (which justified interning Japanese Americans in detention camps during World War II) and to make up for past instances of specific discrimination (which justified court-ordered affirmative-preference programs in states like Alabama).

The issue of sex discrimination has caused the Court a great deal of difficulty. During the 1970s, the states considered but refused to ratify an Equal Rights Amendment (ERA) for women. Should the Court conclude from this that women are not entitled to equal protection? The Court refused to come to that conclusion. In the 1970s the Court decided that sex discrimination was covered by the concept of equal protection and that women (and men) were generally entitled to not be discriminated against because of their sex. At the same time, the Court had to review a number of laws that were designed not to discriminate against women but to discriminate in their favor, in an effort to make up for past discrimination by society. The Court came up with a test that was in between the difficult strict-scrutiny test used for race discrimination and the easy rationality test used for everything else. The Court said that discrimination by governments based on gender would be allowed if it served an "important" government objective instead of a "compelling" one. Compensating for past societal discrimination, while not compelling, was judged to be important, and therefore a number of laws were allowed to stay on the books because the Court believed they helped to make up for past societal discrimination against women.

Both women who have sat on the Supreme Court, Sandra Day O'Connor (appointed by President Reagan in 1981) and Ruth Bader Ginsburg (a Clinton appointee in 1993) have expressed their displeasure with this "lesser standard" for gender-based discrimination. While it has allowed the Court to legitimize programs that arguably help women, it also leaves the door open to discrimination that can hurt women. It is assumed that at some point in the future these two justices will move the Court in the direction of viewing discrimination based on gender as equivalent to discrimination based on race.

The Civil Rights Act of 1964 was passed to make discrimination based on race or sex (or religion or national origin) illegal. Title VII outlawed discrimination by most employers (and was amended in 1972 to include state and local government employers as well as private companies). Other titles outlawed discrimination in a variety of other contexts. For example, the practice common in the South of not allowing African Americans to eat at public lunch counters became illegal. While people debated whether or not a law such as this could be effective, the weight of the legal system came down on social practices that had been commonplace for a century. By the early 1990s it was almost incomprehensible that at one time there had been Whites Only restaurants and public bathrooms throughout the South.

Something else happened that was equally dramatic. Between the Civil War and the 1960s the South had been a backwater of American society. It was significantly poorer than the rest of America because large corporations had little or no presence. With the advent of civil rights, it became legitimate to locate facilities in the South, and Atlanta, Georgia, became the major metropolitan area that it is today. Other parts of the South blossomed overnight once major corporations moved in to take advantage of lower wages and less powerful labor unions. In a very real sense, the economic development of the South came about only because Congress passed the Civil Rights Act of 1964, a statute that many southern senators and representatives did everything they could to stop.

Something else happened in the 1960s and 1970s that changed the face of urban America. The Supreme Court made it clear that whatever it might take, even if it meant forced busing, formerly segregated public school districts would become racially integrated. The Court also decided that busing to achieve racial integration would not cross school-district boundaries. Forced busing to achieve racial integration inside urban school districts combined with no busing across school-district boundaries led to the increased segregation of America. Middle-class white families fled to the suburbs in large numbers, leaving the urban center to poor minorities. By the mid-1990s most school districts had achieved an integrated status, but very few white children went to school with a significant number of black children. It was also still true in the 1990s that the best predictor of the quality of education a child had received was the color of his or her skin. While social scientists have argued that the net result of forced busing has been to increase rather than decrease racial segregation in both schooling and housing, there was nothing the justices of the Supreme Court could do about that. Intentionally segregated school districts had to be integrated, and there was no other choice open to the Court except to force that integration by whatever means it had at its disposal.

Forced busing to achieve racial integration that increases racial segregation and race discrimination that is judged by different rules when compared with sex discrimination have been more than a little frustrating to the average citizen. What are the rules and what do we do now?

THE ACTORS

Throughout most of the last quarter of the twentieth century the courts have distinguished among three very different actors. The first has been the federal government. Courts, particularly the Supreme Court, have recognized the fundamental fact that the major force pushing America forward in the area of civil rights has been the federal government. Until June 1995 the Supreme Court was generally unwilling to interfere with the other branches of the federal government that were charged with making and enforcing the law in this area.

At the same time, state and local governments have been seen very differently. Often, during this period, the entities doing the most to resist change have been cities and states. States like Alabama and cities like Birmingham, Alabama, have been dragged kicking and screaming into federal court in order to enforce federal civil rights laws and the Equal Protection Clause of the Fourteenth Amendment. Of course, the South was not the only part of America that resisted the desires of the federal government in this area. For example, no city opposed forced busing to achieve the racial integration of public schools more than Boston, Massachusetts.

The third major group of actors has been the thousands of private companies across America that in many ways have been caught in the middle. For many businesspeople, the struggle has been not to resist or embrace civil rights and affirmative action but to figure out exactly what they were expected to do. They have simply wanted to be told what it was they were supposed to do so they could get on with the business of making money. Many asked only that whatever burden they had to suffer be placed on their competitors so that the economic battlefield would be level. Their complaint has been that the legal system has not provided them with clear guidance concerning what they could or should do in this area.

One of the problems with discussions of affirmative action throughout the last quarter of the twentieth century has been the unwillingness or inability of those involved in the discussion to be more specific about what exactly they are talking about when they use the phrase "affirmative action." Throughout the rest of this book we will endeavor to avoid that problem. Affirmative-preference programs are coming to an end for a variety of reasons. That does not mean that efforts to achieve affirmative recruitment and affirmative fairness must also end. On the contrary, as preference fades away, fairness must take its place if the ultimate goal of a truly integrated society is to become a reality.

THE DIFFERENCE BETWEEN CIVIL RIGHTS AND AFFIRMATIVE ACTION

It is also important to realize that civil rights and affirmative action are not the same thing. Put simply, achieving civil rights requires an effort by American society to remove factors such as race and gender from the society's decision-making processes. Affirmative action, to the extent that it means affirmative preference, accomplishes just the opposite. It attempts to force decision-makers to take race or sex into account in order to achieve a goal such as faster integration or greater diversity. America has been particularly confused about this. Millions of American employers will gladly tell anyone who will listen that they are "equal opportunity–affirmative action" employers. The only problem with that is they cannot be both. Equal opportunity means ignoring race, while affirmative action means taking race into account. You cannot ignore something and pay attention to it at the same time.

This confusion pervades the society. In America's college classrooms, court decisions that were concerned with civil rights are discussed under the heading of affirmative action and vice versa as if the two terms were interchangeable. They are not. Before we can begin to discuss affirmative action, we have to come to grips with what civil rights means, and has meant, in America's history.

2

FROM SLAVERY TO CIVIL RIGHTS

One of the biggest problems in any discussion of affirmative action is the unwillingness, or inability, of many to separate affirmative action from civil rights. Civil rights was a goal many Americans worked toward for over two centuries. Affirmative action is a modern invention.

THE PROBLEM OF SLAVERY

For the white men who wrote the U.S. Constitution in 1787, the existence of slavery was just one of many problems they had to face in forming a new nation. They realized that there was clearly a contradiction between having fought a revolution in the name of making men free and owning slaves. Many political leaders, such as Thomas Jefferson and James Madison, believed that it would be in the long-term best interest of the new country to end slavery as quickly as possible, but they were unable to create a mechanism to accomplish that goal. The authors of the Constitution decided to leave the issue for another day. Instead, it was decided, for the purposes of apportioning seats in the House of Representatives, that slaves would "count" as three-fifths of a person. This had the result of acknowledging the institution of slavery in the Constitution and of granting greater political power to white men who owned slaves than to those who did not.

As the 1800s progressed, it became clear that the United States was fast becoming two nations, one slave and the other free. While the population of the free states grew faster than that of the slave states, giving the free states the advantage in the House of Representatives, a balance of power between the two groups was maintained in the Senate. This balance was threatened when Missouri asked to be admitted as a slave state in 1818. In February 1819, Representative James Tallmadge of New York introduced a bill that would have admitted Missouri as a state but ended the importation of any more slaves into Missouri and required that all slave children in Missouri be freed at the age of twenty-five. This bill had passed in the House but not in the Senate when Congress adjourned in March 1819. The two major political parties at the time were the Federalists and the Democrats. The Federalist party had been in decline since George Washington left the White House, and many felt that slavery was just the issue to revive it. The Democratic party realized that the faster it could get past the issue of slavery in the territories, the better it would be for its political future. In 1820, Congress passed a series of laws that came to be known as the Missouri Compromise. First, to balance Missouri, a slave state, in the Senate, Maine was admitted as a free state. Second, slavery was outlawed in the territories above the line of Missouri's southern boundary. This meant that the Kansas Territory would be free, while the Arkansas Territory would be slave.

The political implications of the Missouri Compromise were enormous. The Federalist party ceased to exist, replaced first by the Whigs and then by the Republicans. It became clear to many that as had been demonstrated in the debate over the admission of Missouri, the one issue that could defeat the Democrats at the polls, at least in the North, was that of slavery. In 1854 the Kansas-Nebraska Act repealed the Missouri Compromise, allowing new states to decide for themselves whether they would be slave or free.

DRED SCOTT

While Congress had, in the final analysis, refused to stand up against the institution of slavery, many hoped that the Supreme Court would take the lead. Opponents of slavery decided to bring a test case before the Court involving the slave Dred Scott. Dred

Scott had been sold to Dr. John Emerson, an army surgeon living in St. Louis, Missouri, in 1834. Dr. Emerson took Scott with him to the free state of Illinois and then into the free territory of Wisconsin. When Emerson died in 1843, he left Scott to his widow, who moved to New York, leaving Scott with his former owners, the Blow family. Henry Blow, who would later help to found the antislavery Free Soil party, believed that Scott could be used to attack slavery. He financed a lawsuit in which Dred Scott sued to gain his freedom based on the argument that he had become free when Dr. Emerson took him to free soil in Illinois and Wisconsin Territory. British courts had developed a doctrine to deal with the problem of slaves who were brought into British territory where slavery was illegal. The British judges ruled that once slaves entered free territory they were forever free. The U.S. Supreme Court could have simply ruled that this doctrine did not apply in the United States. The Court did that and more.[1]

While it is difficult to understand exactly what a majority of justices ruled (there were eight different opinions covering more than two hundred pages), the basic conclusion was clear. The justices ruled that the Missouri Compromise had been unconstitutional. Slave owners could take their slaves anywhere they wanted in the territories. The federal government did not have the power to "take away" that private property by declaring the slaves to be free simply because they set foot in something Congress had called free territory. In his opinion, Chief Justice Roger Brooke Taney discussed at length the inherent inferiority of the black slave. He said that the states and the federal government did not have the power to grant citizenship to former slaves. This decision made it clear that as far as the Supreme Court was concerned, the only way to end slavery in the United States was with a constitutional amendment. Given the power of the slave states in the Senate, such an amendment would never pass, barring a civil war. Of course, a civil war soon followed.

THE CIVIL WAR AND CONSTITUTIONAL AMENDMENTS

President Abraham Lincoln signed the Emancipation Proclamation on January 1, 1863, proclaiming that all slaves living in the territory held by the Confederate forces were free; thus, as the Union army advanced, it could free slaves and enlist them in the Union army. Lincoln's proclamation also turned the Civil War into a war about slavery, which kept the British, who considered themselves the champions of the world antislavery movement, from joining the Confederate states as an ally. Whether or not President Lincoln had the authority to simply declare that slaves in a particular section of the country were free was a question lost in history. Given the Supreme Court's decision in the *Dred Scott* case, it is difficult to imagine that the Supreme Court would have ruled that he had any such power. Of course, the question was moot after the passage of the Thirteenth, Fourteenth, and Fifteenth amendments to the Constitution. The Thirteenth Amendment, ratified in 1865, outlawed slavery. The Fourteenth Amendment, ratified in 1868, said that the states could not "abridge the privileges or immunities of citizens" or deprive any person of "life, liberty, or property, without due process of law." It also guaranteed that no state could "deny to any person within its jurisdiction the equal protection of the laws." The Fifteenth Amendment, ratified in 1870, said that the right to vote could not be withheld from someone simply because he had once been a slave.

THE RECONSTRUCTION CIVIL RIGHTS LAWS

From 1865 to 1875, Congress passed a number of civil rights laws designed to guarantee the rights of the newly freed slaves. The Civil Rights Act of 1875 said that everyone should be able to enjoy "inns, public conveyances on land or water, theatres, and other places of public amusement" without regard to their "race" or "color." Many Americans, including some legal scholars, felt that Congress had gone too far with this provision. They believed that it did not have the authority under the Thirteenth and Fourteenth amendments to control whether or not private businesses discriminated on the basis of race.

In 1876 the Republican party nominated the governor of Ohio, Rutherford B. Hayes, as its presidential candidate, while the Democrats nominated Samuel J. Tilden, the popular "reform"

governor of New York who had destroyed the famous corrupt
Tweed gang in New York City. Tilden's reputation for honesty,
combined with the corruption scandals of President Ulysses S.
Grant's administration, gave the Democrats their best chance to
win the White House since the end of the Civil War. When the
electoral votes had been counted, Hayes appeared to be the winner,
but there were charges that the ballot boxes in South Carolina,
Florida, Oregon, and Louisiana had been stuffed to guarantee his
victory. Congress created an electoral commission of fifteen highly
respected men to determine who had won in those four states. In
early 1877 the commission voted, eight to seven, that Hayes was the
winner in all four states and therefore the next president.

It is generally believed that a backroom deal was struck
between Republicans and Democrats. Hayes would be the next
president of the United States, and in return the Republicans
would end Reconstruction in the South and forget about civil
rights for former slaves. Federal troops, which had been stationed
in the capitals of the southern states since the end of the Civil War,
were withdrawn.

Meanwhile, five different cases challenging the constitu-
tionality of the Civil Rights Act of 1875 worked their way toward
the Supreme Court. These cases were consolidated in 1883 into one
case which the Court called the *Civil Rights Cases*.[2] The Supreme
Court voted, eight to one, that the Thirteenth and Fourteenth
amendments did not give Congress the power to pass a law that
forced private businesses to "accommodate" black citizens. The
Court ruled that the Fourteenth Amendment applied only to the
actions of states when it said that "no state shall make or enforce"
laws which discriminate. Justice Joseph P. Bradley, writing for the
majority, also ruled that the Thirteenth Amendment did not give
Congress the power to control the actions of private individuals. It
simply ended the institution of slavery. Supporters of the law argued
that the Thirteenth Amendment gave Congress the power to
abolish "the badges" of slavery and that this included requiring inns
and other places of public accommodation to serve blacks equally
with whites. Eight justices did not agree. Only Justice John
Marshall Harlan dissented, arguing that the Thirteenth Amend-

ment did give Congress the power to prevent private individuals from discriminating on the basis of race.

While many of the civil rights laws passed between 1865 and 1875 remained on the federal statute books, they were no longer enforced after the "deal" of 1877 and the decision of the Supreme Court in 1883.[3] Southern states then passed a variety of laws, commonly called Jim Crow laws, which limited the right of blacks to vote or to mingle with whites in theaters, restaurants, and on railroad cars. Whereas the Civil Rights Act of 1875 had tried to enforce integration in places of public accommodation, these laws enforced segregation. Black Americans continued to vote primarily for the Republican party until 1932, but they received little in return.

SEPARATE BUT EQUAL

While it might have appeared that laws requiring racial segregation violated the Fourteenth Amendment because they clearly amounted to action by state governments, the Supreme Court did not see it that way. The 1896 case of *Plessy v. Ferguson* involved a man who had been arrested for violating a Louisiana law that required railroads to provide "equal but separate accommodations" for "white and colored" passengers and required the passengers to obey such restrictions.[4] Mr. Plessy was arrested when he tried to sit in the Whites Only coach. The Supreme Court refused to overturn Louisiana's "separate but equal" law because the majority of justices did not feel that the concept of equal protection in the Fourteenth Amendment could be used to force a "commingling of the two races upon terms unsatisfactory to either." The majority ruled that the Fourteenth Amendment did not prevent states from passing laws that required the separation of the two races in schools, theaters, and railway carriages.

Once again Justice Harlan was the sole dissenter. He argued that the Constitution should be "color-blind" and that any regulation that turned simply on a person's race must be seen to violate the Equal Protection Clause of the Fourteenth Amendment. Justice Harlan not only argued the general principle; he also tried to show that such a rule could prove harmful even to white people.

For example, he pointed out that under the Louisiana law a white man would not be allowed to have his "colored servant" with him in the same coach and that this would clearly be an inconvenience to the white passenger.

Justice Harlan's argument fell on deaf ears, and the doctrine of separate but equal was born. Something that neither the majority of justices nor Justice Harlan felt it necessary to discuss was that the man in question claimed to be "seven-eighths Caucasian and one-eighth African blood." Apparently, even if a person was the least bit black, he could be kept out of the Whites Only railroad car. Decades later, in the debate over affirmative action, the same issue would arise again: How "black" is "black enough"?

THE SUPREME COURT TAKES THE LEAD

By early in the twentieth century it appeared that both political parties were content to abandon the civil rights agenda altogether. On the eve of World War I, President Woodrow Wilson issued an order segregating the U.S. military by race. Between the end of the Civil War and the beginning of World War I the military had been one of the few institutions that could be considered integrated. Now that would no longer be true.

In 1932 black Americans switched their party allegiance from the Republican to the Democratic party. Eleanor Roosevelt became the symbol in the minds of many of the hope that progress could be made in the area of civil rights; but during the administration of Franklin Roosevelt that hope went unrealized. The military remained segregated, and no new civil rights laws were passed. Roosevelt's winning coalition included southern whites along with northern blacks, and he could not afford to alienate either group. He argued that after the Depression had ended and World War II had been won, the Democratic party would turn to the issue of civil rights for black Americans.

At the same time, the Supreme Court was becoming dominated by liberal Democrats and there was progress in one area: education. During the 1930s and 1940s, the NAACP (National Association for the Advancement of Colored People) worked through the courts to achieve more racial integration in education.

However, during those two decades, the NAACP did not challenge the doctrine of separate but equal; instead, it presented the Court with a series of cases in which it was clear that separate was *not* equal. For example, in the 1938 case of *Missouri v. Canada,* Lloyd Gaines, a black man, argued that he had been denied even a separate-but-equal education when Missouri refused to admit him to the whites-only law school but offered to pay his tuition at a law school outside Missouri.[5] Seven justices of the Supreme Court ruled that this did not meet the requirements of separate but equal. Missouri could either build a separate-and-equal law school for blacks or admit Lloyd Gaines. In 1950 a unanimous Supreme Court ruled that the efforts of Texas to build such a law school for blacks were clearly a failure.[6] The black law school in Austin had 5 professors, 23 students, and 16,500 volumes in the library. The white law school at the University of Texas at Austin had 16 professors, 850 students, and 65,000 volumes in the library. The University of Texas Law School was ordered to admit blacks on the same basis as whites.

Encouraged by these results, the NAACP decided to challenge the doctrine of separate but equal in public education. With Thurgood Marshall as lead counsel, the case of *Brown v. Board of Education* was argued and reargued over a period of two years.[7] Finally, Chief Justice Earl Warren was able to write a unanimous decision bringing an end to separate but equal in public education. The justices ruled that separate schools created a "feeling of inferiority" for black students and for that reason violated the Fourteenth Amendment. The *Brown* decision was followed by three decades of social unrest as federal courts wrestled with how to bring about racial integration in formerly segregated public school systems. The racial segregation of the society increased as whites fled to the suburbs, leaving the inner-city schools to blacks and other minorities.

NEW CIVIL RIGHTS LEGISLATION

When John Kennedy won a narrow victory over Richard Nixon in the 1960 presidential election, it was clear to everyone that without a solid black vote Kennedy would not have been elected. At the same time, he faced the dilemma Franklin Roosevelt had faced: The votes of southern whites were also essential to his election. Demonstrations by people of all races for action on the civil rights agenda increased dramatically, culminating in the march on Washington, D.C., on August 28, 1963. At least a quarter of a million people in person, and millions more on television, heard Martin Luther King Jr. give his famous "I Have a Dream" speech. He said that he had a dream that one day the "sons of former slaves and the sons of former slaveholders" would be able to "sit down together at the table of brotherhood."

In 1964, Congress passed a civil rights act which outlawed discrimination based on "race, color, religion, sex, or national origin" by private employers or by those who owned and managed places of public accommodation, such as restaurants and inns.[8] Mindful of the fate of the Civil Rights Act of 1875, Congress based its authority to pass such a law not on the Thirteenth Amendment, but on its power to regulate interstate commerce. This act created the Equal Employment Opportunity Commission (EEOC), but the commission was given no real power to enforce the law. This act was followed in 1965 by a Voting Rights Act which eliminated most of the obstacles that had been created to limit black voting in the South, such as literacy and good-character tests.[9] In 1968 the Supreme Court overturned its decision in the *Civil Rights Cases,* deciding in *Jones v. Alfred H. Mayer Co.* that the Thirteenth Amendment did give Congress the power to outlaw racial discrimination by private individuals and businesses, whether or not they had anything to do with interstate commerce.[10] This decision breathed new life into the civil rights laws that had been passed during the decade after the Civil War.

The Civil Rights Act of 1972 usually gets very little mention in any discussion of the history of civil rights laws—a significant oversight. The act accomplished much that could not have been achieved in 1964. With several years of voting-rights enforcement and the obvious impact of new black voters in the South, it was no longer "politic" to oppose civil rights legislation. Moreover, everyone was beginning to see that society did not crumble with the integration of lunch counters and places of employment.

The Civil Rights Act of 1972 was intended to make up for some of the shortcomings of the 1964 act. In particular, the law made the federal government the overseer of every hiring and promotion decision made by state and local government. While this provision would have been unthinkable in 1964, eight years later it was accepted with little debate. The new act also gave the EEOC power to file lawsuits for poor plaintiffs who could not afford to do so on their own. While organizations such as the NAACP had filed some important class-action lawsuits to end discrimination, they simply did not have the resources that the EEOC had to bring about wholesale changes in the way major companies hired, fired, and promoted.

THE CIVIL RIGHTS ACT OF 1991

For a quarter of a century after the passage of the Civil Rights Act of 1964, the Supreme Court expanded the reach of the law with decisions that made it easier for victims of discrimination to sue and win. Then, in 1989, the Supreme Court handed down five decisions that appeared to limit the rights of victims of discrimination.[11]

In *Price Waterhouse v. Hopkins,* Ann Hopkins complained of sex discrimination when she was not made a partner in the accounting firm of Price Waterhouse. It was clear that while Hopkins was the victim of "sex stereotyping" (the partners did not think that she acted as women are supposed to act), the firm argued that it had other legitimate reasons for denying her a partnership. The Court divided over how to deal with these kinds of "mixed motive" cases. While the more liberal members argued that discrimination should be considered present if sex or race played "some" role in the decision-making process, a majority of the justices ruled that discrimination could be found only if sex or race was a "substantial factor" in the decision.

In *Wards Cove Packing Co. v. Atonio,* the plaintiff argued that the mere fact that very few minorities occupied higher-paying jobs at a salmon cannery in Alaska should be enough to prove discrimination. A majority of the Court ruled that a plaintiff in a civil rights case must prove that qualified minorities had applied for the jobs and had been turned down for illegitimate reasons. The justices felt that if the simple lack of "enough" minorities in a job category were considered proof of discrimination, employers would be forced to institute racial quotas in order to avoid lawsuits for civil rights violations.

In *Martin v. Wilkes,* the Court ruled that white firefighters who had not been a part of an earlier lawsuit against the city of Birmingham, Alabama, could sue for discrimination which they believed they suffered when the city agreed to hire and promote more black firefighters. The Court ruled that because these white firefighters had not been a party to the original lawsuit filed by the black firefighters, they were not bound by the agreement worked out between the black firefighters and the city and approved by the judge.

In *Lorance v. AT&T,* women complained when a union contract was changed in a way that reduced their seniority. The old rule had been that anyone moving from one job to another could take their seniority with them. The women believed that when it became clear that many women with long seniority were moving into higher paying jobs where they would have more seniority than the men who generally held those positions, the rule was changed to make seniority job-specific. The women lost their case when the Supreme Court ruled that they had waited too long to file their lawsuit.

Finally, in *Patterson v. McLean Credit Union,* Brenda Patterson, a black woman, sued her employer for racial harassment. The issue was whether she could sue under the civil rights acts passed soon after the Civil War and be eligible for more damages, or was she stuck with the Civil Rights Act of 1964. The Supreme Court ruled that she was stuck with the Civil Rights Act of 1964.

In the Civil Rights Act of 1991, Congress modified or overturned these five decisions. The act made it possible for people like Brenda Patterson to sue for racial harassment under the old civil rights acts at the same time they sued under the Civil Rights Act of 1964. The act made it clear that people like Ann Hopkins could win if they were able to show that race or sex was a "motivating factor" in the decision, even if it was not a "substantial factor." The act also made it possible for people like the women employees of AT&T to wait and still sue for civil rights violations. As for the white firefighters of Birmingham, Alabama, the act said that people could not sue to set aside a court-approved civil rights agreement if they had been given notice that a decision was about to be made and they had an opportunity to object. The act did not overturn the *Wards Cove* decision. Congress agreed with the Court that a lack of minorities or women in a particular job category is not proof of discrimination. Generally, plaintiffs would have to prove that a "particular employment practice" caused the lack of women or minority employees because it kept them from being hired even though they were qualified to do the work. Individual plaintiffs would have to prove that they applied for the job and were turned down for discriminatory reasons that had nothing to do with job performance.

THE POLITICS OF CIVIL RIGHTS

Throughout two centuries of American history, efforts to achieve civil rights were tied directly to the politics of the nation. The Missouri Compromise was as much a compromise between the Northern and Southern wings of the Democratic party as between Democrats and Federalists. When it became clear that the slavery issue could be used to create powerful opposition to the Democratic party, that party had an incentive to solve the immediate problem and get slavery off center stage. When the Republican party finally came along in the 1850s, dedicated to the end of slavery, it soon replaced the other non-Democratic parties in American politics.

In 1877, when the Republican party realized that in order to maintain power it would have to leave the civil rights agenda behind, it did so quickly and completely. Since black voters had nowhere else to go, it was not in danger of losing the black vote. The Republican party apparently felt that it was inevitable that the Democratic party would regain control of the South as soon as restrictions on white voting were lifted after Reconstruction. This significant southern presence meant that the Democratic party would also have a strong incentive to stay away from civil rights.

That by 1991 the vast majority of senators and representatives were in favor of a new civil rights act speaks volumes about the changes that had occurred in American politics. By the 1990s it was simply not legitimate to be "against" civil rights. This was true for both Republicans and Democrats. President Bush threatened to veto the Civil Rights Act of 1991 but changed his mind when it became clear that more than two-thirds of the senators and representatives were prepared to override his veto.

Changes in the civil rights laws, particularly the voting rights laws, have had a very real impact on political outcomes. In the 1980s both Democrats and Republicans agreed to amend the Voting Rights Act to encourage the creation of "safe seats" for minority candidates. Nothing exemplifies the result of this change in the law so much as the congressional delegation from Georgia. In 1990 the Georgia delegation consisted of nine Democrats (one of them black) and one Republican, Newt Gingrich. In 1994, after new district boundaries had been drawn, only the three "minority only" congressional districts sent Democrats to Congress. The victory of the Republican party in 1994 had very little to do with the "Contract with America" and a lot to do with the new congressional-district boundaries in the South. In 1965 the delegation from the old Confederacy to the U.S. House of Representatives consisted of ninety white Democrats, sixteen white Republicans, and no minorities. In 1995 the delegation from the Confederacy consisted of forty-two white Democrats, sixty-six white Republicans and seventeen minorities.

CONGRESSIONAL REPRESENTATION IN THE CONFEDERACY

	1965	1985	1995
White Democrats	90	72	42
White Republicans	16	43	66
Minorities	0	2	17

On June 29, 1995, the Supreme Court voted, five to four, in *Miller v. Johnson,* that race may not be the "predominant" factor in drawing district boundaries.[12] That decision threw out the Congressional districts of Georgia.

As these statistics show, changes in civil rights laws have had a concrete impact on the politics of the United States. At the same time, by the 1990s, most people were in favor of civil rights. The days when it was "politic" to resist civil rights had gone with the wind. Civil rights meant political equality, social equality, and increased economic opportunity for people who had long been the victims of discrimination. Civil rights, however, did not mean instant economic equality. Some argued that this "flaw" of civil rights legislation had to be overcome as quickly as possible and that the best way to do so was through the use of affirmative action. Some believed that affirmative action could do quickly what civil rights laws would take too long to do: bring economic equality to long-discriminated-against minorities.

3

THE SECRET AGENDA

Affirmative action deserves to be called the "stealth policy." No other public policy owes so much of its existence to obscure appropriations bills, bureaucratic rules, and presidential orders. After thirty years, it is still true that no federal statute actually attempts to deal with the general issue of affirmative action. The Civil Rights Act of 1991 simply said that nothing in the act should be interpreted to affect affirmative action that is in "accordance with the law." A cynic could well ask: What law? Whose law? When did Congress pass a law about affirmative action?

While we could debate when affirmative action really began, it makes sense to go back to the summer of 1941 and a conversation between President Franklin Roosevelt and A. Philip Randolph, the president and founder of the Brotherhood of Sleeping Car Porters, the most powerful black labor union of the time. According to legend, Randolph threatened to hold a mass march on Washington, D.C., in July if Roosevelt did not do something concrete for black Americans. What Randolph wanted was for the federal government to pressure defense contractors to hire more black workers. Roosevelt formed the Fair Employment Practices Commission (FEPC) in response. The commission worked throughout World War II to ensure that black people received a fair shake from defense contractors. Because the entire nation was mobilized for war, anyone who could work could find a job, so it is difficult to judge the success or failure of the commission. After the war the commission was eliminated.

AFFIRMATIVE-ACTION TIMELINE

1941 A. Philip Randolph convinced President Roosevelt to create the Fair Employment Practices Commission to increase black employment by defense contractors.

1948 President Truman signed Executive Order 9980, creating the Fair Employment Board within the Civil Service Commission to increase minority employment in the federal government.

1961 President Kennedy signed Executive Order 10925 requiring federal contractors to take "affirmative action" to hire more minority employees.

1964 President Johnson signed the Civil Rights Act of 1964 and appointed Vice President Humphrey to head the Council of Equal Opportunity.

1965 President Johnson gave a speech at Howard University calling for "equality as a result," and signed Executive Order 11246, putting the Labor Department in charge of affirmative action by federal contractors.

1970 President Nixon and Secretary of Labor George P. Shultz created the Philadelphia Plan to integrate building trades in Philadelphia.

1972 President Nixon signed the Civil Rights Act of 1972. A proposed amendment calling for the end of affirmative action was defeated in the Senate.

1977 President Carter signed the Public Works Employment Act, requiring 10 percent of federal funds given to state and local governments for public works to be spent on Minority Business Enterprises. Bert Lance signed Circular A-46, creating a list of those ethnic groups eligible for affirmative action.

1978 The Supreme Court approved of affirmative action by state universities in the case of *Regents of the University of California vs. Bakke.*

1979 The Supreme Court approved of affirmative action by private employers in the case of *Steelworkers v. Weber.*

1980 The Supreme Court approved of affirmative action by the federal government in the case of *Fullilove v. Klutznick.*

1985 President Reagan considered amending or rescinding Executive Order 11246, but he did not.

1990 President Bush vetoed the Civil Rights Act of 1990, calling it a quota bill.

1991 President Bush signed the Civil Rights Act of 1991.

1995 The Regents of the University of California ended affirmative action programs that gave preferences based on race. President Clinton said he would "mend" but not "end" affirmative action.

It is important to put the conversation between Roosevelt and Randolph into the context of the times. This was not a black leader asking the president to do something to jump-start new civil rights laws with some kind of affirmative action. There were no new federal civil rights laws to set in motion. Instead, it was much more like the kind of conversation that black political leaders had had over the decades with big-city bosses in cities such as Chicago: "My group helped you get elected, and now we want a piece of the action." In a city, such pressure might result in more city jobs for black residents. For the president in 1941 it meant making certain that blacks got a share of the new jobs being created in defense industries. The FEPC was as much in the business of guaranteeing that a constituency of the Democratic party got a "payoff" from the elections as it was in encouraging "fair" employment practices.

In 1948, President Truman signed Executive Order 9980, which created a Fair Employment Board within the Civil Service Commission. The announced purpose of the board was to ensure that minorities, particularly African Americans, got a fair chance to obtain federal jobs. The board disappeared soon after President Eisenhower took office. Again, while there was certainly some idealism involved, there was also some politics. A Democratic president was putting in place a policy to help a constituency.

The Republican president ended that policy after an election in which the Democratic coalition proved it was not strong enough to hold on to the White House.

As vice president, Lyndon Johnson was clearly interested in improving the economic plight of the average black American. At the Texas State Society's inaugural ball in January 1961, Johnson was introduced to Hobart Taylor Jr., a black attorney from Detroit. Johnson asked Taylor to help draft an executive order for President Kennedy's signature. The next day, Taylor and two men who would become Supreme Court justices, Abe Fortas and Arthur Goldberg, wrote an executive order that would attempt to reinstate President Truman's goal of including more black Americans in the federal bureaucracy and President Roosevelt's intention of encouraging more federal contractors to hire minorities. Executive Order 10925 used the phrase "affirmative action" for the first time. Taylor said he chose the phrase "affirmative action" rather than "positive action" because it was alliterative.

The order merged two obscure committees into the President's Committee on Equal Employment Opportunity. This committee became primarily a platform for Lyndon Johnson's Plans for Progress program, which attempted to persuade big companies with large federal contracts to hire more black workers. While it was strictly voluntary and we have no way of knowing how much real impact it had, it was certainly viewed by black political leaders as a step in the right direction.

In 1963, President Kennedy sent a civil rights bill to Congress; after Kennedy's assassination, President Johnson made passage of a civil rights bill his first priority. One argument against the bill was that it would create an incentive for reverse discrimination against whites. Sen. James O. Eastland of Mississippi complained that given a choice between hiring a white or a black worker, both with equal qualifications, employers would hire the black worker. In order to placate such critics as Senator Eastland, a variety of provisions were added to and removed from the bill. Section 703(j) was put in to make it explicit that nothing in the bill required employers to "grant preferential treatment" to anyone. This section was added specifically to persuade southern politicians, such as Senator Eastland, that the bill would not result in "reverse discrimination" against whites. Another interesting thing happened: In an effort to kill the bill, opponents amended it to outlaw discrimination based on "sex" as well as race, religion, and national origin. The bill passed, anyway.

It would be difficult to overestimate the impact the Civil Rights Act of 1964 had on America. It outlawed discrimination in employment and public accommodation. Almost overnight the Whites Only signs came down across the South. Other laws, including a voting rights act, changed the political landscape of America. Suddenly, politicians in such places as Georgia and Mississippi were forced to think about the black vote in their districts.

On June 4, 1965, President Johnson gave the commencement

address at Howard University, a predominantly black institution in Washington, D.C. He asked this question: "Is it reasonable to start a race between two runners, one of whose legs are shackled at the beginning of the race and unshackled halfway into the contest and declare a fair ending without adjusting for the handicap?" But how would we adjust for the handicap? President Johnson had a suggestion. Using a phrase drafted by a young Daniel Patrick Moynihan, he said: "We seek...not just equality as a right and a theory but equality as a fact and equality as a result." But how do you get equality as a result? It was clear to anyone looking at America in the summer of 1965, particularly after the riots in primarily black urban slums such as Watts, that simply making discrimination illegal was not going to produce equality.

On September 24, 1965, President Johnson signed Executive Order 11246, which required companies that contracted with the federal government "to act affirmatively" to guarantee that employees were not treated differently because of their race. (Sex was added a couple of years later.) As amended, it ordered federal contractors to "take affirmative action to ensure that applicants are employed, and that employees are treated during employment without regard to their race, color, religion, sex or national origin." But who would enforce this new requirement?

In February 1965, Johnson created the President's Council on Equal Opportunity, headed by Vice President Hubert Humphrey. During the spring of 1965, Johnson ordered the vice president to come up with a program to ensure that federal contractors complied with antidiscrimination laws. Humphrey proposed that this function be carried out by the President's Council on Equal Opportunity. Johnson seemed to endorse this idea but later changed his mind. It has been suggested that his aides felt that establishing such a high-profile job in the White House would draw controversy. Whether that was the prime consideration or not, the president ultimately decided to abolish the council with Executive Order 11246. The job of ensuring that government contractors lived up to the dictates of the civil rights laws would fall instead to the Labor Department and ultimately to the Office of Federal Contract Compliance (OFCC).

By creating the OFCC, Johnson had entrusted the goal of ensuring that federal contractors actually took affirmative action to people with the power to write federal regulations. From that moment on, any company with more than fifty employees and more than fifty thousand dollars in federal contracts became subject to the power of the OFCC. The office began to draw up regulations, and while the president and the nation turned their attention to the Vietnam War, the OFCC began to tell contractors how to fire, hire, and promote. During Johnson's presidency, the OFCC did not require employers to come up with "goals and timetables," but it did begin to look at the numbers. Edward Sylvester, the first director of the OFCC, has said that he moved in this direction because businesses asked him for some kind of concrete guidance. The only way to give them specific rules to follow was to talk about numbers.

The original idea of affirmative action in Executive Order 11246 was that employers would aggressively seek out qualified minority applicants and then make sure they were treated fairly in the employment process. The text of the order was concerned with affirmative recruitment and affirmative fairness, not affirmative preference. At the same time, in the late 1960s, most employers had no idea how to implement a program of affirmative recruitment and affirmative fairness. Realistically, it was probably not possible for them to do so, given the legacy of decades of discrimination. So they asked for guidelines, and the bureaucrats, who also like numbers, were only too happy to oblige.

The political element must not be ignored. While President Johnson could argue that he was doing something to make civil rights a reality, he was also benefiting his constituency. With Executive Order 11246, President Johnson could point to something concrete that he, as president, had done to help minorities and women move into the workplace.

It was President Richard Nixon and his appointees who moved the OFCC into the business of affirmative preference. In 1970, Nixon's secretary of labor, George P. Shultz, created the first major "quota" plan, the Philadelphia Plan. It required building contractors in Philadelphia who were receiving federal funds to hire more minorities, particularly African Americans. Using the threat of lawsuits as the stick and the promise of federal money as the carrot, the Nixon Labor Department was able to accomplish in a few months what most people thought would take a decade: major progress in integrating the Philadelphia building trades. Nixon and his bureaucrats were so happy with the results of the Philadelphia Plan that they wrote up regulations for all the other federal contractors subject to Executive Order 11246, which, for the first time, specifically called for goals and timetables.

It was the perfect solution to what many sensible people saw as an almost intractable problem. After decades of intentional exclusion from higher-paying building-trade unions, apprenticeship programs, and construction jobs, pushing for progress would have taken many years and many lawsuits. Union locals and employers in every major city would have had to be sued at significant expense. By putting the process under the table, so to speak, the job could be done much more quickly and quietly.

While the Labor Department was working on private contractors, other federal departments and agencies began pressuring state and local governments. The Department of Health, Education, and Welfare (HEW) asked school districts and colleges to seek out and promote "by the numbers." School districts with mainly white teachers and minority students felt the most pressure to do something about the imbalance. Lost in the big push to get more minorities into the classroom and into administrative positions was any concern with the quality of teaching. Everyone seemed to take it for granted that minority children would somehow learn better from teachers who were also minorities. Also, it was assumed that minority teachers and administrators would act as role models for minority students in a way that white teachers could not. In some cities, such as San Francisco and New York, this meant demoting or not hiring a lot of Jewish administrators and teachers to make room for the new "favored groups."

What was really happening was not lost on the American Jewish community. In the magazine *Commentary* (published by the American Jewish Committee), several articles in 1972 demonstrate a real awareness of what this new affirmative-action effort would mean to Jewish Americans, who would simply be classed as "white." In the January 1972 issue, Earl Raab wrote an article entitled "Quotas by Any Other Name."[1] He described the program of the San Francisco School Board to "deselect" 125 white administrators, many of them Jewish, to make room for administrators who were from a "correct" ethnic group. The list consisted of eight favored ethnic groups: blacks, Chinese, Japanese, Koreans, American Indians, Filipinos, Spanish surname, and other nonwhite. Earl Raab objected to what he saw as a giant step backward for Jewish Americans, arguing that one of the marks of a free society is the ascendance of "performance over ancestry."

Ultimately, the San Francisco School Board decided not to deselect the administrators, but instead to make it clear that no more "white" people would be made administrators until the sought-after minorities held enough administrative positions. Earl Raab argued for affirmative recruitment and affirmative fairness instead of affirmative preference. He did not object to seeking out "qualified" minority applicants or providing training programs for "qualifiable" minority applicants. What he objected to was the use of affirmative preference to make it difficult, if not impossible, for white (and Jewish) applicants to compete.

In the next issue of *Commentary*, Paul Seaburg wrote an article chronicling the transition from combating discrimination to using discrimination to favor certain formerly disadvantaged groups.[2] He described how Labor Department Order No. 4 required federal contractors to use goals and timetables to increase the number of minorities and women in their companies. He also discussed how HEW was doing the same thing with universities that received federal funds. HEW was requiring universities to hire more "underutilized" people.

Finally, in the October 1972 issue of *Commentary*, Elliott Abrams pointed out that the Civil Rights Act of 1972 had given the EEOC the power to file lawsuits and to regulate state and local governments.[3] While the law did not require quotas, it was clear to Abrams that employers would get the message written between the lines of new EEOC regulations.

When the Civil Rights Act of 1972 was being considered, something else happened that received little notice outside Washington, D.C., but was very important to the future of affirmative action. A group of senators tried to amend the act to outlaw any kind of affirmative-action programs that discriminated in favor of someone because of race or sex. They argued that the 1964 act outlawed discrimination both against and for minorities and that this clear purpose was being ignored. Their amendment was easily defeated with a vote of sixty to thirty, which was taken as a clear signal from Congress that while the elected representatives did not feel they could actually authorize affirmative action, they were in favor of it. Some of the politicians who would argue against affirmative action in the 1990s voted against the amendment that would have outlawed it in 1972.

The successful defeat of anti–affirmative-action amendments in Congress in 1972 was not lost on the justices of the Supreme Court. While Congress apparently did not have the courage to deal openly with the issue of affirmative preference, it was clear that the Court could do so without fear that Congress would move to overturn its decisions with legislation.

There was something else happening in the early 1970s that went unmentioned. The list of ethnic groups that needed affirmative action specifically included Chinese and Japanese Americans. While it is certainly true that both ethnic groups had suffered from racial discrimination in the past, particularly in California, where they were concentrated, both groups were doing quite well without affirmative action. In fact, from 1950 to 1970 these two ethnic groups jumped from close to the bottom of the "charts" to very near the top. By the early 1970s, they were doing better than English or German Americans, the two largest components of "white" America, based on almost every measure. They had a higher average family income, a higher net worth, and a higher percentage of people with advanced degrees. How did they do it? For one thing, they found themselves concentrated in California while California was booming economically. During those two decades, anyone who invested in real estate or a business in California was very likely to see their investment increase greatly in value. Chinese and Japanese Americans did invest, and they did well. Also, during those decades, it was possible to get an excellent college education for almost nothing from the state of California. Chinese and Japanese Americans took advantage of the opportunity in large numbers. They demonstrated that formerly disadvantaged minorities could do very well in a society that offered full employment, rising real estate values, and a free college education, as California did for several decades after the end of World War II.

The presence of Chinese and Japanese Americans on the list of favored groups told anyone who was watching that something was going on besides just trying to get everyone to the same starting line. By every objective measure these two groups were ready to compete without any special preference by the 1970s. If the goal of affirmative action was to make up for past discrimination by society until the disadvantaged groups could compete on their own, then these two groups should never have been put on the list.

With the coming of President Carter, affirmative action moved into high gear. While the president himself stated that he was uncomfortable with any kind of discrimination, whether in favor of or against people, because of sex or race, many in his administration were committed to affirmative action, which manifested itself in various forms. For example, there are many ways to calculate underutilization of a particular group. If we are talking about hiring someone for an unskilled job, then it is not unreasonable to ask what percentage of the working-age population in a particular city is of a particular ethnic group. If we are talking about a skilled job, this kind of gross comparison makes little sense. Yet it is the kind of calculus the Carter administration increasingly subjected people to.

The Carter administration also moved into the area of setting aside some government contracts or grant programs for minorities and women. The idea got a major boost in 1977 when Congress passed the Public Works Employment Act, which required that at least 10 percent of all federal funds granted to state and local governments to build public works projects be used to "procure goods and services" from minority business enterprises (MBEs). An MBE was any business that was at least 51 percent owned by "Negroes, Spanish-speaking, Orientals, Indians, Eskimos, and Aleuts." It was not exactly clear how Congress came up with this particular list of ethnic groups or how it decided that 10 percent was the right amount rather than 5, 15, or 20. The law did prevent the participation by MBEs "whose access to public contracting opportunities is not impaired by the effects of prior discrimination." The law did not explain how it would be determined which MBEs had or had not been impaired by the effects of prior discrimination.

With the passage of this law and the determination of the Carter administration to move aggressively in this direction, the number of federal programs that set aside contracts or grants for people who fit the list multiplied. By the 1990s, 162 federal programs would grant some kind of preference based on race or sex, most without any authorization from Congress.

There was, of course, a political dimension to all of this bureaucratic activity. President Nixon had hoped to break some minority voters away from the Democratic party with his aggressive affirmative-action program. The bureaucrats in the Carter administration, many of whom were women and minorities, set out to prove that no one could outperform the Democrats with respect to affirmative action. After all, these groups were part of the Democratic "core" constituency. How could the Democrats hope to retain the White House without the votes of women and minorities?

On May 12, 1977, Bert Lance, then director of the Office of Management and Budget (OMB), signed Circular A-46, which set out how it would be decided if someone was of the preferred race. An individual would have to have at least one grandparent who was "American-Indian, Alaskan, Chinese, Indian, Japanese, Korean, Filipino, Mexican, Puerto Rican, Cuban, Central or South American, Samoan, Pacific Islander, Spanish culture, or black African." Under this regulation, Indians from India were included for the first time. We have no way of knowing if this was intentional or simply a mistake. (Once "Indian" becomes "American Indian," then Indian must mean from India, or at least that is the logic of lawyers.)

By the end of the 1970s the affirmative-action battle was being fought on three main fronts: college campuses, where affirmative action meant admitting more women and minority students and hiring more women and minority faculty; personnel offices, where affirmative action meant hiring more women and minorities; and government agencies, where affirmative action meant setting aside some portion of every program for people who fit the desired set of characteristics. The emphasis was already moving away from trying to make up for past instances of discrimination and in the direction of attempting to create in every small part of society a microcosm of the larger society. The watchword became "diversity" rather than discrimination. This new emphasis on diversity made it even more difficult to know how to count by the numbers. Do you want every organization to look like America in general or a state or metropolitan area in particular? How do you deal with the fact that a large percentage of African Americans and Hispanic Americans are under the age of eighteen?

Throughout most of the 1970s, the Supreme Court played the game by deciding not to decide. For example, in 1971 the Court refused to hear an appeal from a decision that upheld the Philadelphia Plan. In 1974 the Court decided not to hear the *DeFunis* case. Marco DeFunis had been denied admission to the University of Washington Law School; because he won at the trial-court level, the university had been ordered to admit him. By the time the Supreme Court was ready to decide his case, Marco DeFunis was about to graduate, and the justices decided it made no sense, given this fact, to render a decision on whether or not he should have been admitted in the first place.

At the end of the 1970s the Supreme Court did decide three major affirmative-action cases and in each case affirmative action won.[4] In the 1978 case of *Regents of the University of California v. Bakke*, the Court decided that a state university could use race and sex as admission criteria in order to create a more diverse student body. In the 1979 case of *Steelworkers v. Weber*, the Court decided

that private employers could introduce affirmative-action programs, even if they had not been ordered to do so by a judge,
without violating the federal civil rights laws. In the 1980 case of
Fullilove v. Klutznick, the Court decided that Congress had the
power to set aside a percentage of federal contracts for minority-
owned businesses.

The publicity surrounding these three Supreme Court decisions ensured that the media would devote a great deal of time to
the issue of affirmative action in 1978, 1979, and 1980. Millions
of white men, whether or not they had any personal experience
with affirmative action, were made to feel that the federal
government was out to get them. President Nixon had hoped that
affirmative action would drive a wedge between two traditional
Democratic party constituencies: minorities and white blue-collar
workers. That was one of the reasons he decided to go after the
building trades in the Philadelphia Plan. He assumed that minorities would see this as a Republican initiative that did something
concrete to help them and vote Republican in response. What
happened in the presidential election of 1980 was the reverse.
White blue-collar workers saw affirmative action as a Democratic
plot to deprive them of their jobs. These angry white-male voters
were called the "Reagan Democrats," and most analysts agree that
they made Ronald Reagan's victory possible.

When Reagan became president, everyone assumed that he
would do something about the affirmative-action problem, or at
least that is what the Reagan Democrats hoped. Numerous ideas
were put forward soon after his election in 1980. Some suggested
getting rid of all affirmative-action programs. Reagan's first
attorney general, William French Smith, said that quotas were
"discredited and ineffective." Others suggested changing the regulations so that only larger companies with a minimum of 250
employees and $1 million worth of contracts would be subjected
to the "goals and timetables" regulations of the OFCC. That
would have eliminated 75 percent of the 200,000 companies that
were under the control of the OFCC in the early 1980s.

In the April 19, 1982, issue of *Fortune,* Daniel Seligman
explained that affirmative action would probably survive Ronald

Reagan and that if it did it would survive anything.[5] While everyone from Clarence Thomas, the conservative black head of the EEOC, to William Bradford Reynolds, the conservative white assistant attorney general for civil rights, said that quotas should be eliminated, the person who really counted, Secretary of Labor Ray Donovan, was against getting rid of goals and timetables. Anyone wanting to reduce or eliminate the OFCC would have to go over his head, and Seligman suggested that this would not happen. Moreover, while the business community was unhappy with some of the affirmative-action regulations, they were not clamoring for an end to the OFCC or for repeal of Executive Order 11246.

When Ronald Reagan was reelected in 1984, many people thought that he would finally do something about affirmative action. The following year, there was a well-publicized fight between Donovan and Ed Meese, the attorney general over affirmative action. The newspapers and magazines of that period indicate that everyone thought Reagan's second term would bring about the end of affirmative action or at least the end of Executive Order 11246. In August 1985 there were "strong rumors" in Washington, D.C., that Reagan would at least amend Executive Order 11246. In the September 16, 1985, issue of *Fortune* Anne Fisher explained why it would not happen.[6]

What the battle over affirmative action during the summer of 1985 revealed was one of American business's dirty little secrets: *big business likes regulations.* Regulations generally provide larger enterprises with an advantage over smaller ones, which cannot afford to hire the army of bureaucrats needed to comply with the sea of regulations. In the case of affirmative action, almost every big business had spent a great deal of time and money creating an affirmative-action bureaucracy to match the federal bureaucracy at the OFCC. They understood what was expected of them and were simply not willing to go off into some new unknown world. Moreover, they had found that federally sanctioned goals and timetables gave them a real edge when someone suggested he or she might file a lawsuit based on race or sex discrimination.

The average business with federal contracts could argue not

only that they did not discriminate but also that they were working with the federal government to bring about affirmative action. In a survey of 128 CEOs of major corporations, 122 said they would continue some kind of "numerical objective" program even without government regulations. The discussion ended when the National Association of Manufacturers came out in favor of affirmative action.

Congress also got into the act, as usual, through the back door. On December 7, 1985, a letter signed by two hundred members of Congress was sent to President Reagan urging him not to "tamper" with affirmative action.

During Reagan's second term, his administration exhibited a double-pronged approach to affirmative action. Executive Order 11246 and the OFCC were the real engines of affirmative action in America, and they continued to be just that. At the same time, the Justice Department asked various cities that had settled discrimination lawsuits by agreeing to implement some kind of affirmative-action plan to reconsider that decision. None of tthem did. The Reagan administration had found a way to have its cake and eat it, too. It got some credit in the press for being against affirmative action philosophically while not actually doing anything about it practically. The news media never emphasized that all President Reagan had to do to stall the major engine of affirmative action was to amend or rescind Executive Order 11246.

President Bush followed Reagan's lead. He vetoed the Civil Rights Act of 1990, calling it a "quota bill." He signed the Civil Rights Act of 1991 only after he was convinced of two things: that it would not bring about quotas and that if he vetoed it two-thirds of both the House and Senate were prepared to override his veto. President Bush projected the image of the quota buster, and yet he did nothing about Executive Order 11246 or the OFCC.

President Clinton apparently had no desire to examine the issue of affirmative action or to do anything other than follow in the footsteps of the Carter administration. Throughout 1995, Clinton made it clear that he would just as soon leave the entire issue alone.

Through more than two decades, from 1972 to 1995, Congress continued its "stealth strategy." While many individual senators or representatives railed against affirmative action, particularly if they needed it as an issue in a close election, nothing of substance ever seemed to happen in Congress that would weaken it; instead, Congress provided "secret" support. For example, when the Federal Communications Commission (FCC) suggested that it would reexamine its affirmative-action regulations, Congress placed a provision in the appropriations bill that forbade any of the money appropriated to the FCC to be spent reexamining affirmative action. Since the passage of the Civil Rights act of 1972 many citizens have asked their elected representatives to provide some guidance on the issue of affirmative action, but none was forthcoming. Instead, Congress sent out "signals of support" for the general issue without ever having to face up to hard questions such as how long affirmative action would continue and which groups actually belong on the list of minorities to receive special help?

The American people were never treated to a fair debate over the issue by their elected representatives. Whether the leadership of the House and Senate thought that the "people" were too ignorant or too prejudiced to be able to understand the complexity of this issue is not clear. What is obvious is that Congress deserves as much of the credit, or blame, for the current state of the law in this area as the president and the bureaucrats. Both the executive and the legislative branches of the federal government encouraged the development of affirmative-preference programs throughout the society with little regard to either the impact these policies were having or the extent to which people were willing to support them. It was one policy concerning which no one wanted to know what the will of the people was, nor did they have any desire to honor it.

With a few exceptions, the media were perfectly willing to go along with the secret agenda by calling anyone who questioned the accepted policy on affirmative action a racist or an opportunist—still the standard media policy when, on July 20, 1995, the University of California Board of Regents voted to end affirmative action in the university system. On Sunday, July 23, the television media made it clear that affirmative action was not to be attacked. While Gov. Pete Wilson was given a few minutes to explain the decision on ABC's *This Week With David Brinkley,* Jesse Jackson was allowed to shout him down on the same program. Meanwhile, on other networks, a variety of officials appeared on news programs to question either this action of the board in particular or Governor Wilson's motives in general. On the CBS show *Face the Nation,* Leon Panetta said that any move to end affirmative action was a "terrible mistake" and might result in a loss of federal grants and contracts for the entire state of California. On the NBC show *Meet the Press,* Senator Bill Bradley charged that Governor Wilson was "stirring the pot of racial turmoil," while William J. Bennett told NBC that Wilson had signed twenty-one bills on affirmative action before changing his mind. Bradley and Bennett suggested that Wilson was taking this stand at this time simply because he was running for president. Bennett called it "political opportunism." In October, Pete Wilson dropped out of the race for the Republican presidential nomination.

THE POLITICS OF RACE

Throughout the history of affirmative action there was something else going on besides the idea of helping to improve the lot of minorities, and that something was politics. President Roosevelt created the FEPC to hold on to his electoral coalition. President Truman did the same when he created the Fair Employment Board, which President Eisenhower allowed to disappear for similar political reasons.

President Nixon moved affirmative action into high gear in an effort to break minorities away from the Democratic party. President Carter worked hard to prove that the Democrats could "deliver" on affirmative action better than the Republicans. President Reagan won the presidency as a result of the "backlash" by white voters against what they felt was discrimination against them.

Gerald Ford, to his credit, refused to engage in the politics of race. However, it was not lost on anyone that Jimmy Carter won the election easily in 1976. We may never know for sure whether Gerald Ford and his advisers made a philosophical decision not to use the politics of race or simply felt that doing so would not help in the campaign against the governor of Georgia.

George Bush turned the politics of race into an art form. No one who saw his Willie Horton commercial can forget the image of dangerous black men being released from prison by Governor Dukakis to claim other victims. The message was clear: Michael Dukakis is a bleeding-heart liberal, and bleeding-heart liberals only care about black people. They don't care about the rest of "us." The campaign slogan could have been: Vote for George Bush, He Cares About White People. George Bush won easily.

We have every reason to believe that President Bush planned to employ the politics of race in 1992. His veto of the Civil Rights Act of 1990, which he called a quota bill, was going to be the first volley in the politics of race. His problem was that his own political party pulled the rug out from under him; while he was trying to build a record of fighting quotas and protecting whites, the Republicans in Congress fashioned a new civil rights bill that could gain enough votes to override a presidential veto. Bush was trapped. If he vetoed the bill, he would be overridden and appear to be out of step with his own party. He decided to claim victory and sign the bill.

We will never know if the politics of race would have worked for Bush in 1992. Ross Perot set the agenda for the campaign debate, and race and affirmative action were not on his list. Bush lost the election.

Of course, the politics of race in general and of affirmative action in particular were not limited to presidential politics. In 1990 many commentators thought that Jesse Helms of North Carolina might lose his Senate seat. Then his campaign unleashed the "worried hands" commercial. Television audiences in North Carolina saw only a pair of white hands on the screen. The hands crumpled up a piece of paper as a voice said: "They had to give it to a minority because of a racial quota." It was clear from the visual cues and the verbal message that this was a middle-aged white man who had been rejected for a job because of his race. Helms was reelected. He proceeded to concern himself with American foreign policy, not affirmative action. From 1990 to 1996 there was no great campaign in the Senate by Helms to end affirmative action. Why not? Possibly because he figured he might need the issue again in 1996.

The June 5, 1995, issue of *U.S. News & World Report* called affirmative action "the mother of all wedge issues." The article was about the California Civil Rights Initiative. Begun by Tom Wood (a white man who was denied an academic job because of affirmative action) and Glynn Custred, professor at California State University at Hayward, the California Civil Rights Initiative has as its stated goal to bring an end to affirmative action in California. It would outlaw race and gender preferences in college admissions, government contracting, and government employment. It states simply that the state of California and its subdivisions may not use "race, sex, color, ethnicity or national origin" to either discriminate against, or grant preferential treatment to, anyone in the operation of the state's "system of public employment, public education or public contracting." This is essentially a quote from the Civil Rights Act of 1964 except for the phrase about "preferential treatment."

Tom Wood and Glynn Custred are happy to explain the origin of their drive to end affirmative action. In 1991 the California legislature passed a bill (vetoed by Governor Wilson) which encouraged state universities to make sure that their "graduating classes" reflected the state's ethnic makeup. To Wood and Custred this act, sponsored and passed by Democrats, was the last straw. It is one thing to give people a chance but quite another to force universities to dumb down the course content, or whatever else it would take, to make sure everyone graduated. It is a sentiment with which many people in California apparently sympathize. Polls conducted in early 1995 showed that two-thirds of voting-age Californians supported the initiative, including from 40 percent to 50 percent of blacks and Hispanics.

That the Democratic party and other groups, such as the NAACP, simply do not get the message is amazing. The attitude of the Democratic party seems to be that there have been flaps about affirmative action in the past and that this one will blow over just like the rest. The NAACP apparently hopes to use the attacks on affirmative action to revitalize a sagging membership.

President Clinton appears to hold similar beliefs. In the spring of 1995 he discussed changes in affirmative-action policies with the leaders of the California Democratic party. According to published reports, Willie Brown, the black speaker of the California House, told Clinton that any weakening of affirmative action would cause him to lose the support of the Democratic party in California. Clinton thought about this threat for several months and apparently decided to cave in. On July 19, 1995, in an address delivered at the National Archives, he pledged his support for the continuation of business as usual in the area of affirmative action. He was applauded by those assembled to hear the speech. That applause may sound the death knell for his political campaign in 1996. Looking back over three decades, the politics of race have only helped the Republicans and hurt the Democrats. Excerpts from his speech exemplify the confusion many Americans have about affirmative-preference programs. Clinton said he would not allow affirmative action to "hurt white men," and he would "not stand for quotas." But when a white man is the low bidder on a public works project that is given to another company simply because the owner of that company is of the right sex or race, how can we say that the white man is not hurt? If 10 percent of public works contracts are set aside for minority-owned firms, how is that anything other than a quota? That is a question for which Clinton did not have an answer.

The politics of affirmative action are strange. We can only assume that Bill Clinton had his eye on California, a state that he must win to remain president, when he spoke of maintaining affirmative action. But polls show that supporting affirmative preference is something less than one-third of voting-age Californians are prepared to do. Half of those who are supposed to benefit from the programs do not want them. For whatever reason, they reject the idea of preference even if they might be a recipient. This fact is one of the most interesting in the equation of racial politics in America. Many of the minorities and women who are supposed to benefit from preference say they are opposed to preference programs.

Some might ask what the problem is. It is that affirmative action has exacted, and continues to exact, a high cost for the society in terms of racial antagonism. Also, there have been victims of affirmative action, and many of them have been the people it was designed to help.

4

VICTIMS OF AFFIRMATIVE PREFERENCE

When we hear people say that affirmative action is not about quotas and lower standards, we have to wonder if they are misinformed or intentionally trying to mislead. When we hear others contend that there are no victims of affirmative action, we have to wonder where they have been living and who they have been listening to. It is particularly annoying to hear government officials and politicians, who clearly know better, pretend that affirmative action has never hurt anyone.

QUOTAS

A large number of affirmative-preference programs have quotas. Some programs call them goals; others, quotas. But generally they amount to the same thing. A fixed percentage of the contracts awarded or the employees hired will be of the desired race or sex. It is a disservice to the affirmative-action debate to suggest otherwise.

Government contracting is one area in which quotas rule the day. Federal laws passed to appropriate money for building highways have required since 1977 that "not less than 10 percent" of the money be paid to companies that are owned by women or minorities. In 1977, Congress provided a particular list of minorities that were entitled to special treatment. This law stated that "Negroes, Spanish-speaking, Orientals, Indians, Eskimos, and Aleuts" could take advantage of the set-aside program. In 1991 the $151 billion transportation act stated that the 10 percent quota was to go to "small business concerns owned and controlled by socially and economically disadvantaged individuals." Women and minorities are presumed under federal regulations to be in that category.

Across the United States, anyone who cared to find out about quotas had only to look at how states and cities spent their contract dollars. In Los Angeles, general contractors who are building stations for the new subway system are required to subcontract at least 25 percent of the business to companies that are owned by women or minorities. One contractor put in a bid on a station that called for only 23 percent to be spent on such subcontractors. He was not awarded the contract, even though his bid was hundreds of thousands of dollars lower than the next-lowest one. That contractor sued the city. If 25 percent was a "goal," then 23 percent and a large savings should have been enough to win the contract. That it was not means that 25 percent was a quota.

In other cities the quota is 10, 20, or as much as 30 percent. These contract set-aside programs are the most glaring quotas on the affirmative-action landscape, although there are many others. For example, the U.S. State Department demands that "not less than 10 percent" of the money used for construction go to "minority contractors." The U.S. Defense Department tries to give 5 percent of its over-$100-billion-a-year procurement budget to socially and economically disadvantaged individuals, which means, for all practical purposes, that almost every penny which is not allocated to large weapons systems goes to minority- or women-owned firms.

There are more than 150 affirmative-preference programs in the federal government (162 by one count). The National Institute of General Medical Sciences reserves about 4 percent of its research budget for "educational institutions with a significant

proportion" of minority students. That meant that in 1994
million went to fund research in colleges such as Mor
School of Medicine in Atlanta, Georgia and California State
University in Los Angeles, California. In providing grants for
teacher training, the U.S. Department of Education gives "special
consideration" to "historically black colleges and universities" and
to schools with at least 50 percent minority students. The
Environmental Protection Agency (EPA) requires anyone receiving
a grant to make a "positive effort" to use "minority-owned
business sources of supplies and services." The Department of
Agriculture encourages those who receive rural housing grants to
use "minority banks."

By far the main engine for the creation of quotas in the United
States is the OFCC. It requires every business with more than fifty
employees and more than fifty thousand dollars worth of contracts with the federal government to prepare goals and timetables
for creating a more diverse workforce. This office supervises more
than 90,000 companies at any one time (the number apparently
rises and falls depending on the year and has been reported to be
as high as 400,000.) These companies employ about one-fourth of
the private workforce in the United States. The OFCC has the
power to completely bar a company from doing business with the
federal government, but most of the time it contents itself with
reviewing hiring practices and ordering the payment of back
wages to people it believes a contractor would have hired if it were
serious about meeting the goals. The office conducts about four
thousand audits of federal contractors a year. In one audit the
OFCC decided that Solectron, a California company, had not
hired enough minorities.[1] In the judgment of the OFCC, nine more
minorities should have been hired. The company agreed to pay
$237,000 in back wages and made job offers to the nine minority
workers who had applied and been turned down. Of course, the
bureaucrats argue that these goals are not the same as quotas, but
it is difficult to see the difference. Companies who do not hire
"enough" of a particular kind of person are subject to a variety of
penalties. While large contractors can absorb the costs of providing all the paperwork required by the OFCC, small businesses are

at a significant disadvantage. The OFCC manual on how to create a system of goals and timetables is seven hundred pages long.

The OFCC says they have goals, not quotas. A survey by *Fortune* magazine asked CEOs specific questions about goals and timetables, and 54 percent said that they had "goals but no numerical quotas," while 18 percent said their companies had "specific quotas for hiring and promotions."[2]

One of the most pervasive quota systems is supervised by the Small Business Administration. The Small Business Act allows government agencies to grant contracts of up to $5 million for manufacturing and $3 million for services to companies that are owned by socially and economically disadvantaged individuals. Remember, a woman or a minority, regardless of his or her actual economic circumstances, is assumed to be socially and economically disadvantaged. Over five thousand companies participated in this program in 1994. Forty-six percent were owned by blacks; 23 percent, by Spanish speakers; and 21 percent, by Asians. A handful were owned by white women; another handful, by white men who were able to prove that they were also disadvantaged. Companies are allowed to remain in this program for up to nine years even if they are no longer "disadvantaged," but it's a program that has had trouble sharing the wealth. In 1994 over half of the firms "on the list" did not receive any contracts; a small number of firms received the lion's share of the business.

THE QUALITY OF PEOPLE HIRED

Whether the search for a job candidate of just the right race or sex results in lower standards is a difficult question to answer. It has certainly resulted in different standards. In many cases, a good argument can be made that the old standards kept out women or minorities without any evidence that they were work related. At the same time, it is ludicrous to argue that affirmative preference has never resulted in hiring people who were less able to do the work. We have only to look at a few of the hundreds of reverse-discrimination lawsuits which have been filed over three decades to find ample evidence that the best candidate was not always chosen for the job, at least not until a judge got involved.

Perhaps the most famous case of reverse discrimination in America is that of *Walters v. City of Atlanta* (1986).[3] When Dennis Walters, a white male, was six years old, he was taken to visit the Cyclorama in Atlanta, Georgia. The Cyclorama is a large painting, 50 feet tall and 350 feet in circumference, that depicts the Civil War battle of Atlanta. Dennis Walters was so taken with the display that he said he wanted to manage the place when he grew up. During the 1970s the Cyclorama was closed for restoration. When it was ready to reopen in 1981, the city established a list (called a register) of people eligible for the position of director. Seven names were on the register, all white. Dennis Walters was listed as "well qualified" because he had worked for the Georgia Historical Commission and the North Carolina Museum of History. Three of the names were submitted to the parks commissioner, Geraldine Elder, for her consideration, but when she found out that all three were white, she asked for a new register. As an interim measure, Elder appointed a black woman who had campaigned for Mayor Andrew Young as the new director of the Cyclorama. The woman was fired in 1982 for poor performance.

When the new register was created in 1982, Dennis Walters was still listed as a well-qualified applicant. David Palmer, a black man, was first listed as unqualified, but that evaluation was changed to qualified when it came to light that he had two years of experience in "food-product marketing." Palmer was hired instead of Walters. In 1983, Carolyn Hatcher, the new parks commissioner, fired David Palmer when she discovered that in violation of city regulations, he was holding down two full-time jobs. Hatcher then hired Carole Mumford as director. Carole Mumford had been listed as qualified on the 1982 register.

Unlike most white men who have suffered from this kind of reverse discrimination, Dennis Walters sued for race discrimination. The jury found that he was the victim of intentional race discrimination. He was awarded the pay he would have received if the city had hired him in 1981 and was given the job of director of the Cyclorama. The jury also awarded him $150,000 as compensation for the mental anguish that he had suffered. His attorney fees of $60,000 were also paid by the city of Atlanta.

We could discuss dozens of other cases. When the black principal of mainly black South Oak Cliff High School in Dallas fired Norman Jett, the white head football coach, so he could hire a black head football coach, Jett sued.[4] These kinds of affirmative-action programs, as a result of which white people are fired to make way for someone with the right skin color, are particularly disliked by the Supreme Court. Norman Jett was awarded $450,000 in damages and $112,870 in attorney fees.

When the black fire chief of the District of Columbia hired a black assistant fire chief, the five deputy fire chiefs, all white, sued for race discrimination.[5] The fire chief had selected a black battalion chief, which is a level below that of deputy chief. The district judge in the case found that the five deputy chiefs were superior in terms of "seniority, education, and experience" to the black man who received the promotion. The circuit court agreed. The fire chief was ordered to hire one of the deputy chiefs for the job of assistant chief.

The point is that affirmative-preference programs have sometimes meant hiring or promoting people who were not qualified or who were clearly not *as* qualified as people of the "wrong" race or sex. To deny that is to ignore the obvious. Of course, we cannot know how often this has happened or how unqualified such people have been because in the vast majority of cases the victims did not file complaints.

WHO ARE THE VICTIMS?

It is generally assumed that white men are the major victims of affirmative-preference programs. In one poll, 10 percent of white males said that they felt they had lost a promotion because of quotas.[6] Almost every white man who has looked for a job as a college professor since 1975 has been the victim of affirmative preference.[7] A number of books support this finding, including George Roche's *Balancing Act*, Richard Lester's *Antibias Regulation of Universities*, and Frederick Lynch's *Invisible Victims*.

To discuss the victimization of white men is to belabor the

obvious, but there are other victims of affirmative preference. Most of them have not sued because they are themselves women or minorities. Take the case of a black man we will call Joe Doe. Joe was a hard worker, but he lost his job when the small factory where he worked closed down. Joe was more than qualified for a similar job at another factory that constantly advertised for employees, but he could never get a foot inside the door. Finally, Joe filed a complaint with the EEOC. The factory owners defended themselves by pointing to their excellent affirmative-action record. Almost all of their assembly-line employees were both women and minorities: Asian and Latin American women, many of them recent immigrants. The owners had never hired a black man. Why not? Was it because they were prejudiced against blacks? Was it because they were afraid that a black man, particularly one who had worked in a factory setting before, might ask questions about safety regulations or wage and hour rules? Joe Doe did not pursue the case any further. He had come up against the perfect defense to a charge of race discrimination: an affirmative-preference plan with "very good numbers."

Or take the case of someone we will call Rhonda Roe. Rhonda was hired as a college professor by one of the Cal-State campuses in 1989. When she arrived, she found that a group of women held important positions in the administration and were generally considered to be powerful on campus. Some of these women had an agenda that included "dumbing down" the content of the classes as much as possible. The expressed reason for this agenda was to ensure that more minorities would graduate, but Rhonda did not buy this reasoning. First of all, she found that her minority students were generally just as capable of doing the work in her classes as white students. Second, she did not think dumbing down the course content was the way to deal with high dropout rates among minority students. She asked if the problem had ever been studied in a scientific way and received blank stares for an answer. Apparently, the women in power assumed that minorities dropped out because they were too stupid to compete. No one stopped to inquire to what extent socioeconomic factors contributed to the high minority dropout rate. Because Rhonda Roe refused to participate in the general plan to lower the level of instruction, she was labeled a subversive.

During her years on campus Rhonda worked hard to participate in programs designed to aid minority students. She acted as a mentor to a minority female student and worked with many students outside of class. She also called parents who were obstacles to their children's success. For example, one very bright female minority student kept telling Rhonda that she had to miss class in order to run errands for her father. Rhonda called the father and found that this was indeed the problem. Rhonda tried to help her, but without regular class attendance this student, who had mastered English as a second language, was simply not able to keep up.

In her fourth year, Rhonda came up for tenure and was turned down. She decided to wait and ask for a peer-review panel in her fifth year. In the winter of her fifth and final year, a peer-review panel was convened to hear her case. It consisted of two women and one man, all with tenure, all from departments outside Rhonda's. Rhonda presented to this committee all of the evidence she had compiled concerning the three criteria that tenure decisions are supposed to be based on: her service to the university, her teaching performance, and her scholarly research and publications.

The panel also received a five-page, single-spaced memorandum from the dean. This memorandum began by recommending that Rhonda not be given tenure because she had been hired under the affirmative-action program. This was news to Rhonda, and she asked the members of the committee who had hired her about the claim. They told her that she had been the best candidate for the job but was an affirmative-action hire, anyway. How can the best candidate be an affirmative-action hire? Because the department that hired her had been told they had to hire a "woman or minority" for every white man they hired. Since her hiring had been used to "justify" the hiring of a white male (who received tenure the same year Rhonda was denied it), she was therefore an "affirmative-action baby."

The dean's memorandum went on to make plain his major

complaint about Rhonda Roe: that she acted too much like a woman. The peer-review panel's final report said:

> The Dean's reference to Rhonda Roe's personality characteristics:
> "she is a very pleasant person,"
> "breathless ebullience,"
> "demure and retiring nature,"
> "not dynamic or aggressive,"
> "smiles pleasantly,"
> are inappropriate in assessing professional competence.
> The Panel is unanimous on this point.

The peer-review panel recommended that Rhonda Roe be given tenure. They found, with a vote of three to zero, that she met the required level of performance when it came to scholarship; with a vote of three to zero, that she met the required level of performance when it came to service; and with a vote of two to one, that she met the required level of performance when it came to teaching ability. The president of the university, a white man, reviewed all of the documents and denied Rhonda Roe tenure a second time.

Rhonda Roe sent copies of the documents to the board of trustees of the Cal-State system and to the civil rights office of the federal Department of Education and filed a complaint with the California agency charged with ending discrimination, but nothing happened. She talked to several attorneys, none of whom were willing to represent her and take on this particular campus because it had "good numbers."

While Rhonda Roe was being denied tenure, another woman, whom we will call Martha Moe, was granted it. Whereas Rhonda Roe's record of teaching, scholarship, and service was reviewed by several committees and ultimately by a peer-review panel, Martha Moe never even compiled such a record. The president simply signed a piece of paper transforming her instantly from a temporary instructor to a tenured associate professor. You see, the men in the department where Martha Moe taught were trying to fire her. The vice president of academic affairs, a woman, apparently felt that the only way to protect her was to convince the president to take this extraordinary step. Would Martha Moe have received tenure if she had gone through the normal review process? We will never know. No one objected to the procedure, presumably for fear of being called a sexist. Was Martha Moe the recipient of affirmative action or simply the personal friend of someone with power on campus?

Apparently, the dean felt justified in attacking Rhonda Roe in such an obviously sexist way because she did not have the support of the powerful women on campus. Since the women did not want her, he felt free to unleash any kind of attack, no matter how sexist or misleading. In a world where numbers count more than ability, this seems sad but understandable.

Efforts to dumb down the curriculum at the Cal-State campuses bore bitter fruit in 1994, when the University of Texas Law School successfully defended itself before the trial-court judge against a reverse-discrimination lawsuit filed in part by a female graduate from another Cal-State campus. The law school argued that while she had high grades they were from a low-quality college and should not count for much. We have to wonder how many graduates of the Cal-State system will find that their fate has also been sealed by a misguided effort to "accommodate" more minority students. It should not be surprising, then, that two-thirds of the citizens of California would like to end affirmative preference in their state as quickly as possible, before it can do any more damage.

How many Joe Does and Rhonda Roes have been the victims of affirmative action? How often has affirmative action been the cover story for what most people would call favoritism? We will never know. As long as affirmative action, in the form of affirmative preference, is taken as a license to hire or promote anyone with the "right" sex or race regardless of ability, there will be others who will face the problem of being women or minorities and still victims of affirmative preference.

5

THE CONTRIBUTION OF THE SOCIAL SCIENCES

It is incredible to realize how little social scientists in the United States have studied the impact of affirmative-action programs. As John Leo pointed out in *U.S. News & World Report,* "perhaps half a dozen serious books" have appeared on the subject over a thirty-year period.[1] Presumably most social scientists figured it was a no-win situation, given the general attitude in the country that anyone who questioned affirmative action must also be a racist or a sexist. Since social scientists could not know what their research would demonstrate, many of them apparently decided it would be better to leave well enough alone.

STATISTICS CAN PROVE ANYTHING

One of the first problems social scientists have tried to deal with has been the gross misuse of statistics. Thomas Sowell, a conservative black economist at the Hoover Institute, has observed on many occasions over the last thirty years that most of the statistics used to support the need for affirmative action make no sense. They usually compare apples and oranges. For example, as he pointed out in the June 1978 issue of *Commentary,* when you compare the wage level of the "average" Hispanic American with that of the "average" Jewish American you are comparing someone who is, on average, under twenty years of age with someone

61

who is, on average, over forty years of age.[2] Should we be surprised to learn that people over forty make more money, on average, than people under twenty? In that article he pointed out that the average wages of blacks increased in the 1960s, before affirmative action and declined in the 1970s, after affirmative-preference programs were instituted.

One of the best-kept secrets has been that by the mid-1970s, if we looked at college graduates, thirty years of age, living in the same region of the country, race and gender accounted for almost no difference in wage levels. The average thirty-year-old Hispanic college graduate made about the same as the average thirty-year-old white college graduate, who made about the same (a little less, actually) as the average thirty-year-old black college graduate. In his book *Ethnic America,* Sowell stated that much of the apparent difference in family income between ethnic groups could be explained by age, education, and region of the country.[3] He pointed out that while the statistics purported to prove that blacks and Hispanics had lower incomes than whites in general and a great deal less than Jewish and Japanese Americans in particular, what they really proved was that older people have higher incomes than younger people, the educated have higher incomes than the uneducated, and Californians have higher incomes than Mississippians. When he compared young married couples living outside the South, blacks had earned 78 percent of white income in 1959 and 93 percent of white income in 1971. He also found that black people from the West Indies had higher incomes than white people once these adjustments were made.

In other words, Sowell demonstrated in the late 1970s and early 1980s that statistics can prove anything or nothing, depending on what factors are taken into account. Comparisons of working people of the same age, education, and region demonstrated as early as the 1970s that race accounted for, or caused, very little difference. He summarized his findings this way:

> In short, blacks achieved the economic advances of the 1960s once the worst forms of discrimination were outlawed, and the only additional effect of quotas was to

undermine the legitimacy of black achievements by making them look like gifts from the government.[4]

THE CASE OF THE CALIFORNIA PARKS DEPARTMENT

One of the few social scientists to conduct an in-depth study of a government agency's affirmative-action program is Bron Taylor, who reported the results of his research in his book *Affirmative Action at Work.*[5] He studied the California Department of Parks and Recreation by observing its operations, conducting surveys, and interviewing employees. He found that white men and Native-American men were the two groups of employees most opposed to the department's affirmative-action programs. Native-American women and minorities were generally in favor of affirmative-preference programs.

Bron Taylor tells the story of one hiring panel that was made up of a white man, a Hispanic man, and a Hispanic woman. The white man and the Hispanic woman recommended that the job be given to a white man. The Hispanic man recommended a Hispanic candidate. The supervisor, a white man charged with making the final decision, chose the Hispanic man in order to get the "Hispanic numbers up." Taylor describes how the California Department of Parks and Recreation began its affirmative-action plan in 1975 under "pressure" from the federal government. He discovered that the department, after a decade and a half, was still unclear about whether its plan called for quotas or simply tried to increase recruitment and fairness. Although the personnel department emphasized that goals were not quotas Taylor's observations demonstrated that the managers who made personnel decisions viewed the goals as quotas that had to be met. He found that this "lack of clarity" about the true nature of the department's affirmative-action program created tension throughout the organization.

Taylor found that many white male employees were filled with "hostility and disillusionment." He was shocked by the intensity of feeling exhibited by white males, who felt that their careers were being sidetracked in the name of affirmative action. He cited one young white man who almost did not get into the service because of his race and sex who told him: "If I ever get to a place where I have any power over hiring, I will do everything I can to thwart this affirmative-action bullshit."

Taylor suggested that the unwillingness of those in charge of the department to admit that their affirmative-action program was actually an affirmative-preference program, complete with quotas, created even more resentment than if they had just been honest about it. He called for truth in affirmative action, and argued that affirmative preference had not caused those who received the preference to lose their self-esteem, as so many commentators had suggested. Quite the contrary, he found that people who were placed in positions of responsibility and per-formed well had higher self-esteem because they saw themselves succeeding in a difficult job.

PSYCHOLOGICAL EXPERIMENTS

Social psychologists conducted a series of studies throughout the period of affirmative preference, most of which were concerned with the effect of affirmative-preference programs on women; their findings were largely ignored by the media and the general public.

In 1977, Marsha Jacobson and Walter Kich reported their research in an article entitled "Women as Leaders: Performance Evaluation as a Function of Method of Leader Selection."[6] In this experiment, male college students were told they would partici-pate in an experiment. When each male student arrived at the laboratory he found a female student waiting for the experiment to begin. In reality, the female student was a confederate of the experimenters. The male subjects were told that the female student would be the leader in a two-person group. The first group of subjects were told that the decision to make the female student the leader was the result of chance (the experimenter flipped a two-headed coin, and the female confederate called out "heads"). The second group of subjects were told that the female student was chosen to be the leader because she had performed well on a test of ability. The third group of subjects were told that the female student was chosen because she was a female and they needed more female leaders for the experiment to come out even.

The female confederate and the male subject then performed an oral-communication task in which the leader had a picture and attempted to describe it to the follower. In this experiment, the female leader had a picture of dominoes and the male follower had eight dominoes, in front of him. The male follower tried to arrange the dominoes based on the information given to him by the female leader. Of course, the follower could not see the picture. For half of the subjects, the female confederate gave clear instructions, and the group "succeeded." For the other half of the subjects, the female confederate gave unclear instructions, and the group "failed." The experimenters then asked the male subjects to rate their "leader" on a scale of one to nine, one being the lowest rating and nine the highest. Males who had been told that their female leader was chosen because of her sex consistently rated her low, whether the "group" had succeeded or failed. Those who had been told that their leader was chosen at random rated her better, and those who had been told that their leader was chosen because of her expertise rated her best of all.

RESULTS OF EXPERIMENT—RATINGS OF FEMALE LEADER

	Sex	Random	Merit
Success	7.67	8.42	8.92
Failure	3.25	3.92	4.58

The psychologists who conducted the experiment expected such results. According to what psychologists call "equity theory," when people are faced with what they feel is inequity, they try to make changes to compensate for what they see as injustice. If they cannot change the facts, they change their perception of them. In this case, faced with women leaders who were chosen simply because of their sex, the men in the experiment put more of the blame for failure and less of the credit for success on the female's shoulders. On the other hand, when the males believed that the women had been chosen as leaders because of their ability, they were willing to assign them less blame for failure and more credit for success. Since in the real world the evaluations women receive are often made by men, it is clear what impact the existence of affirmative-preference programs are probably having on those evaluations. There is also every reason to believe that the same would hold true if the leaders were minorities and those doing the rating believed they had received their leadership status because of racial preference programs.

In 1982, Thomas Chacko conducted a study of women managers in the Midwest.[7] He gave them a questionnaire that asked how they felt they had been selected for their executive position. They were asked if ability, education, experience, or sex was the reason for the selection. The questionnaire then asked about their satisfaction with work and their feelings about their coworkers.

Chacko found that women who felt they had been hired or promoted because of their sex had significantly less satisfaction with their job and their coworkers than women who believed they had been hired or promoted because of their ability. Women who were convinced that they owed their position to sex rather than ability also had a low level of commitment to the company and experienced a great deal of conflict over their role in the company. Chacko suggested that such findings demonstrated the concrete effect of the stigma women feel when their innate ability has not been the major factor in their success. This stigma leads to low job satisfaction and a decline in commitment to work. There is every reason to believe the same would apply to minorities.

Madeline Heilman, a psychologist at New York University, has conducted several experiments concerning the effect of affirmative preference on women. In 1984 she passed out questionnaires to college-bound high school students.[8] The students were given a description of what it is like to be a sales manager. Some of the students were informed that 8 percent of sales managers are women; others were told that 28 percent are women. Some of the job descriptions indicated that the number of women in this particular job field was due to the effort of companies to "actively recruit and promote competent women whose credentials and education enable success at such a job." In other words, some of the subjects were told that there was a large percentage of women in the field because they had worked hard to succeed on their own merit and employers had engaged in affirmative recruitment, not affirmative preference. Others were told that the high number of women in the field was due to the effort of companies to "create more managerial positions for women as a result of pressures from legal regulations." In other words, other subjects were told that there was a large percentage of women in this field because of an affirmative-preference program created by government. Professor Heilman found that the amount of interest in the job expressed by young women increased if they were told that there were 28 percent women rather than 8 percent women in the field, but only if they were also told that those women had gotten their jobs through merit. Students who believed that the high level of women in this job category was the result of an affirmative-preference program were not any more interested in it even if the number of women was 28 percent instead of 8 percent.

In this experiment Heilman was testing the "role-model theory," which states that if the number of women (or minorities) in a particular job increases they will act as role models, and attract more young women (or minorities) to that particular job. Her experiment suggests that the impact is not as simple as basic role-model theory suggests and that young people who believe their role models got their jobs because of an affirmative-preference program will not be attracted to the field. She concluded: "If the presence of sizable numbers of women is to spark the occupational interest of other women, it is necessary that women not only *be* in particular positions but that they also arrive at them in a particular way—on the basis of merit." In other words, the simplistic notion that society can attract more women and minorities to particular occupations simply by hiring more of both through affirmative preference programs does not hold up under scientific examination.

In 1987, Heilman conducted a laboratory experiment using male and female college students as subjects.[9] In the experiment, when the subjects arrived to participate in the study, they found a student of the opposite sex already waiting to take part in the experiment. The second student was in reality a confederate of the experimenters. The subjects were told that they were going to engage in a communication study. The "leader" would hold a diagram and describe it to the "follower," who would then do his or her best to draw the pattern that the leader had described. Only the leader would be allowed to talk; the follower (a confederate) simply had to draw. The experimenters explained to some students that they had been selected to be the leader of this little two-person group because of merit, based on the results of a test the experimenters had previously given, while other students were informed that they had been selected to be the leader of the little group so that the experimenters would have "enough" women, or men, to play the role of the leader.

At the end of the experiment the drawings were graded, or so the student subjects were led to believe, and the subjects were informed that they had succeeded or failed because their group's drawings were in the "top" or "bottom" 25 percent of all those who performed the task. Of course, the experimenters simply told half of the subjects that their drawings were in the top quarter and the other half that their drawings were in the bottom quarter. Then the subjects were given a questionnaire to rate their own leadership performance and to express interest, or lack of it, in continuing to be a leader.

Professor Heilman and her colleagues found that males who believed they had been a success rated their own performance high whether they thought they had been selected because of merit or simply because the experimenters needed more male leaders to make the experiment come out even. Females who believed they were a success rated themselves high if they thought they had been selected on the basis of merit but low if they thought they had been selected because of their sex. Women who believed they had failed showed the same pattern, rating themselves lower if they thought their sex was the criterion used to select them as leader in the first place. Women who thought they had been selected because of their sex also said they did not want to continue as leaders. Women who thought they had been selected because of merit did express interest in continuing to play the role of leader.

Research suggests that both men and women tend to believe that women have fewer of the skills needed to be a good leader, which presumably robs women of some of the self-confidence that men exhibit in these kinds of experiments. When that self-doubt is increased by telling women they were picked to be a leader only because of their sex, it is "particularly devastating for women." Professor Heilman concluded that "when selected on the basis of preference rather than merit, the women consistently rated their performance more negatively, took less credit for successful outcomes, and were less eager to persist in their leadership roles." In other words, since women begin with doubts about their ability to be good leaders, telling them that they were chosen because of their sex rather than ability only adds to that already existing self-doubt, with negative consequences for the women involved.

In 1990, Heilman reported on another experiment.[10] The purpose of the study was to see if giving females information about their own ability could counteract the otherwise negative effects of telling them that they had been selected because of their sex. In this study both males and females were made leaders in a similar one-way communication study. Some were told that they had been selected on the basis of merit; the rest believed that they had been selected on the basis of their sex. Of this second group, some were told that even though they were being selected on the basis of their sex, they had performed well on a test designed to help select good leaders. Others learned that they did not perform well on this test; still others were not given any information about their test performance.

Female students who believed that they had been selected on the basis of their sex and were given no information about their test performance had a negative view of themselves, as we would expect, given the results of past experiments. However, those who believed that they had been selected because of their sex and also that they had done well on the test had as positive a self-image as those women who were told they had been selected on the basis of merit. Which suggests that women who have good reason to have a high level of confidence in their own ability are not harmed by preference programs but that women who do not have informa-tion which would lead them to believe that their ability level is high are victimized by them.

Finally, in 1991, Professor Heilman reported on a study designed to measure how telling people they were selected on the basis of preference effects the kinds of work that they chose to do.[11] In this study, male and female students were asked to play the role of a financial-services manager. Some were told that they had been selected to play the part of manager because of their ability; others were informed that they had been selected for the part because of their sex. ("We need more men or women to make the numbers come out even.") They were given one student who acted as their subordinate; of course, this "worker" student was in reality a confederate of the experimenters. The subjects were asked to pick one of two tasks to perform in their new role as manager. One task was generally perceived to be much more difficult than the other. Professor Heilman found that women who believed that they had been selected to play the role of manager because of their sex chose to perform the less demanding task. Heilman suggested that "women who believe themselves to have been preferentially selected on the basis of their sex for managerial or other male sex-typed positions often will shy away from the very activities and projects that will give them visibility and facilitate their advance-ment." This avoidance of difficult tasks then leads to lack of self-confidence in women. In other words, a belief that preference accounts for their position leads women to avoid difficult tasks, which is likely to prevent them from moving up the ladder any further, that is, without more preference based on sex.

In 1989, Rupert Nacoste reported on his own experimental research in *Affirmative Action in Perspective*.[12] In his study, men and women were first asked if they thought affirmative action was fair or unfair. A majority of both men and women in the study said they thought it was unfair. The subjects were then given a test of creativity. Half of them were advised that they were selected to continue on in the study because they scored high on the test. The others were told: "When we looked at the test scores, we discovered that we didn't get as many (women or men, depending) as anticipated. Because we wanted to have approximately equal numbers of males and females to do this task, we included some (men or women) whose scores fell below the original minimum score of eighty." The subjects who had been informed that some people of their sex had been allowed into the study with a low score were not told that they were in that group or how far below the 80 level the people who were participating in the study actually scored.

The subjects were then given two computer-controlled brainstorming tasks to perform. They had to come up with as many uses for a burned-out match and an empty coke can as they could in a short period of time. After they had finished, they were asked to estimate how well they had performed the task. The participants, regardless of sex, who felt that affirmative action is unfair and were told that someone had been included in the study so there would be enough people like them, rated their own performance very low. This was true even though their performance was actually higher than average on the tasks studied. In other words, for people who feel affirmative action is unfair, the mere existence of some kind of preference program for "people like them" lowers their own self-evaluation.

It is generally assumed that the only victims of affirmative-preference programs are the white men who do not get the jobs or promotions in question. A decade and a half of experimental research suggests that the number of victims is much larger and includes many women and minority members who do not have very good reasons to believe in their own self-worth. Also, women and minorities who do not believe affirmative-preference programs are legitimate—by most calculations at least half of all women and minorities—are particularly victimized. Not only are they subjected to a policy with which they disagree, but their own self-confidence is lowered as a result.

THE SCAR OF RACE

The most recent published study of survey research with important implications for the future of affirmative-preference policies is the book *The Scar of Race,* written by Paul Sniderman and Thomas Piazza.[13] These social scientists conducted a number of studies that combined some of the qualities of an experiment with the methodology of survey research.

In one study, interviewers asked white people about their opinion of blacks. For half of those surveyed, they were first asked what they thought of the fact that "a nearby state," had reserved a "large number of jobs" in state government for blacks, "even if their scores on merit exams are lower than those of whites." The researchers did not care what their answer to this question was. What they wanted to know was whether or not simply asking this question before asking people about their feelings toward blacks would affect the result. It had a dramatic affect. The "mere mention" of the existence of affirmative preference in some other state caused people to express much lower opinions of black people in general.

RESULTS OF MERE MENTION OF AFFIRMATIVE ACTION

| | Percentage in Agreement | |
	Mention	Not Mention
Blacks are irresponsible.	43	26
Blacks are lazy.	31	20
Blacks are arrogant.	36	29

It is generally argued that people who oppose affirmative-preference programs do so simply because they are racists. This research suggests that some of the racism may go in the other direction. Some people may have become racists "because" of the existence of affirmative-preference programs. The authors concluded that "affirmative action is so intensely disliked that it has led some whites to dislike blacks—an ironic example of a policy meant to put the divide of race behind us in fact further widening it."

The authors found that most whites dislike racial preference in employment and in college admissions. This was true even when supposedly "liberal" whites, such as those who live in the San Francisco Bay Area, were surveyed. At the same time, surveys showed that whites did not fit neatly into the "racist" theory. While a majority opposed affirmative-preference programs and busing of school children to create integrated schools, a majority were in favor of civil rights laws and providing money to help poor blacks climb out of poverty.

They also found that women generally did not support preference programs for women regardless of the country studied. In the United States, 18 percent of women supported preference programs for women, while in Australia the figure was 8 percent and in Germany 15 percent. This study, combined with Rupert Nacoste's finding that women who feel affirmative action is unfair underrate their own level of performance, suggests that most women are probably being harmed by the mere fact that affirmative-preference programs exist in society.

Sniderman and Piazza's research demonstrates that the simplistic view that whites are simply racists and that this explains their opinions and behavior no longer holds up. They argued that while "all public policies designed to assist blacks used to evoke the same reaction from whites, today, social welfare policies and race-conscious policies are evaluated in distinguishably different terms." For example, whites can feel that busing and affirmative-preference policies are unfair and still support antidiscrimination laws and policies that spend money to help the poor. They also found that whites who considered themselves "conservative" were more willing to spend money to help poor blacks than they were to help poor whites. Presumably they felt that whites had a better chance of helping themselves when compared with blacks who still face the affects of racism.

Finally, they found that people were more willing to support affirmative-action programs if they were told that Congress had approved them. In one experiment, people were asked if they favored set-aside programs that reserved some government contracts for minorities. When simply asked the question, only 43 percent of whites favored set-aside programs. When told that Congress had passed a statute authorizing the set-aside programs, 57 percent were in favor of this policy. In other words, white people are more willing to go along with affirmative action if they feel their elected representatives have actually approved of the program.

CONCLUSION

One of the major arguments for continuing affirmative-preference programs is the need to allow minorities and women to break the "glass ceiling" into top positions in business and government. The research which has been conducted in this area suggests that one of the pillars holding up the glass ceiling may be the existence of affirmative-preference programs. Women and minorities who already have self-doubts or who feel affirmative-preference programs are unfair may tend to underrate their own performance and limit their own achievements. Moreover, people who are charged with evaluating them may rate them lower because of the existence of affirmative preference. Finally, the mere existence of affirmative preference may cause some people to be more racist than they would otherwise be.

These research projects also point out the problem with eliminating "some" affirmative-preference programs and not others. If this occurs, these programs will continue to do a great deal of psychological harm to women and minorities with even less offsetting good. The only way to eliminate the effects discussed in this chapter is to bring an end to race- and gender-based preference programs throughout the society. Only then can women and minorities be freed from the psychological burden they bear because of the mere existence of affirmative-preference programs.

6

THE SUPREME COURT
BEFORE BAKKE

In the American legal system, the last word on an issue such as affirmative action usually comes from the Supreme Court. Before we can discuss what the Court has said about the law of affirmative action, we must first delve into the more general area of the law of equal protection. To what extent must government treat people equally without regard to their race or sex? Throughout the history of the United States that has been a very difficult question for the Supreme Court to answer.

FROM THE CIVIL WAR TO WORLD WAR II

As discussed in chapter 2, the Supreme Court's involvement with the issue of slavery and equal protection was not always something for later generations to be proud of. Chief Justice Taney's opinion in *Dred Scott v. Sandford* is an incredible example of the racist ideology of the 1850s.[1] He essentially said that blacks were so inherently inferior that they could never be raised to an equal level with whites. With its decision in *Plessy v. Ferguson* in 1896 legitimatizing the concept of "separate but equal," the Court approved all of the Jim Crow laws that had created a Whites Only and a Coloreds Only world in the South.[2] However, between the Civil War and World War II, not all the decisions were regrettable.

The Fourteenth Amendment says that states may not "deny to

any person" within their jurisdiction the "equal protection of the laws." While that did not mean blacks had the right to ride in Whites Only railroad cars or attend Whites Only public schools, it did mean that they had a right to some level of "political equality." The 1879 case of *Strauder v. West Virginia* involved the conviction of a black man for murder by an all-white jury.[3] Blacks were prevented by law from serving on juries in West Virginia and most southern states. The Court ruled that states could not exclude blacks from juries simply because of their race and threw out the conviction. The Fourteenth Amendment guaranteed blacks some degree of political equality, and that included the right to serve on juries. Of course, even after laws that excluded blacks from serving on juries were repealed, most juries were drawn from the list of registered voters, and a variety of mechanisms kept most blacks from ever being able to register to vote in the South.

In the 1886 case of *Yick Wo v. Hopkins,* the Court ruled that the Fourteenth Amendment protected all people from race discrimination at the hands of government, including Asians.[4] The case concerned a San Francisco ordinance that made it illegal to house a laundry in a wooden building. The announced purpose of the rule was to prevent fires, since laundries had to boil water. However, there was substantial evidence that the ordinance was enforced only against people of Chinese descent. Others were routinely granted an exemption from the rule. A unanimous Supreme Court ruled that the Equal Protection Clause of the Fourteenth Amendment prevented this kind of discriminatory enforcement of what seemed to be a race-neutral law. The Supreme Court would eventually rule that the Equal Protection Clause even protects white people.

THE CREATION OF STRICT SCRUTINY

During World War II the Supreme Court, a majority of whose justices had been appointed by President Franklin Roosevelt, would again face the question of how to deal with intentional race discrimination by government. The 1944 case of *Korematsu v. United States* involved the practice of rounding up Americans of

Japanese descent during the war and sending them to detention camps.[5] These camps were created under the authority of the president as commander in chief not only to prevent sabotage but to protect Japanese Americans from mob violence. In 1944 the issue of whether or not this practice violated the principle of equal protection came before the U.S. Supreme Court. While the Equal Protection Clause of the Fourteenth Amendment applies only to the states, the Court had previously ruled that the Fifth Amendment, which requires the federal government to provide everyone with "due process of law," includes an "implied" Equal Protection Clause.

A majority of the justices ruled that it was constitutional for the military, under orders from the president, to round up Japanese Americans. The Court created what would henceforth be the test for judging whether or not race discrimination by federal, state, or local government violated the Equal Protection Clause. Justice Hugo Black, writing the majority decision, said:

> ...all legal restrictions which curtail the civil rights of a single racial group are immediately suspect. That is not to say that all such restrictions are unconstitutional. It is to say that courts must subject them to the most rigid scrutiny. Pressing public necessity may sometimes justify the existence of such restrictions, racial antagonism never can.

What Justice Black called "rigid scrutiny" later justices would call "strict scrutiny." The strict-scrutiny test came to mean that before racial discrimination would be allowed, government must have a "compelling reason" for the discrimination and must "narrowly tailor" what it does to achieve that compelling reason so it does not do any more harm than is absolutely necessary. A majority of justices ruled in the *Korematsu* case that the new test had been met because protecting the nation in time of war was so compelling.

It was inevitable that the concept of separate but equal would eventually collide with that of strict scrutiny. The collision finally occurred in 1954 when the Supreme Court overturned separate but equal in the case of *Brown v. Board of Education*.[6] Over the years since the Civil War, many states had developed a dual system of public education, one for blacks and the other for whites. In 1954, with the *Brown* decision, a unanimous Supreme Court ruled that the concept of separate but equal "has no place" in public-school education. The justices accepted attorney Thurgood Marshall's argument that segregation alone created a "feeling of inferiority" among black students and for that reason segregation violated the principle of equal protection.

In the years following the decision in *Brown v. Board of Education,* the Supreme Court and lower federal courts struggled with ways to integrate public school systems that had been created to keep the races separate. These dual systems had often required both black and white students to be bused to their respective schools. Some people argued that simply forcing school districts to draw new attendance zones around each school would bring an end to the dual system, with students of all races attending their neighborhood school. However, because of patterns of housing segregation, this would have resulted in very little racial integration in most public schools. The courts decided that in many cases students would have to be bused from one area to another within the school district so that each school could be as racially integrated as possible.

In 1974, with the case of *Milliken v. Bradley,* the Supreme Court had to face the ultimate problem with this policy.[7] As school districts instituted busing to achieve racial integration, white families began to flee to the suburbs. Many urban school districts were left with very few white students as a result. Faced with this fact, the federal district judge in Detroit recognized that the Detroit public schools would never achieve much in the way of racial integration unless white and black children were bused across school-district boundaries, and he ordered such a system of busing to begin. A majority of Supreme Court justices were not willing to go that far. In a decision written by Chief Justice Warren E. Burger, the Court ruled that as a general rule federal judges did not have the authority to order busing across school-district boundaries. As a legal doctrine, this made a lot of sense. There had to be some limit to efforts to force school integration. However, as a public policy, this decision reinforced the pattern of white flight from the major urban centers of America into the surrounding suburbs. If the Court had ruled that children would be bused across school-district lines, the white families might have stayed in the cities, realizing that there was no escape from integrated schools. With the *Milliken* decision, it was clear that they could escape if they could get across the school-district boundary into the nearest "white suburb." Many jobs and much of the tax base went with the fleeing whites, leaving minorities to cope with rising unemployment and all the social problems that come when people cannot support themselves and their families in an urban environment.

Two decades after *Milliken,* the "average" inner city in the United States had become a place with high levels of crime, divorce, infant mortality, and out-of-wedlock births and low rates of high school graduation. As more than one black scholar has pointed out, the black family survived centuries of slavery and a century of so-called separate but equal treatment. But it did not survive the urban ghettos, which became a fact of life for too many African Americans in the 1970s and 1980s.

THE PROBLEM WITH WOMEN

While lawyers and judges debated the effect of the concept of equal protection on black men, everyone accepted the idea that it did not change the facts of life for women. Before 1920, women could not vote in most states, and their ability to own property or hold a job was severely limited. In 1920 the Nineteenth Amendment was ratified, giving women the right to vote throughout the country in all elections. However, there was no Equal Protection Clause in the Nineteenth Amendment. The question for the Supreme Court became: Now that women had the right to vote, should they be treated equally in other ways by government?

In 1923 the question of the equal rights of women arose in the case of *Adkins v. Children's Hospital.*[8] The District of Columbia had a law that set a minimum wage for women but not men.

Minimum wages for men had already been declared unconstitutional by a Supreme Court that believed that most efforts by government at all levels to regulate business violated the Constitution. In this case a majority of justices ruled that in light of the passage of the Nineteenth Amendment, women should no longer be seen as second-class citizens. Justice George Sutherland, writing for the majority, recognized that in some cases "the physical differences" between men and women would have to be recognized, possibly justifying rules limiting the length of time a woman could be asked to work in certain occupations, but there was no reason why women should be "subjected to restrictions upon their liberty of contract which could not lawfully be imposed in the case of men under similar circumstances." In other words, women would have the same right to work for low wages, unprotected by a minimum wage law, that men enjoyed. The justices felt that women should have the same right to the equal protection, and the equal lack of protection, of the laws. Felix Frankfurter, who would later be appointed to the Supreme Court by President Roosevelt, argued the case in favor of the power of governments to set a minimum wage for women.

The battle to change the Supreme Court's mind about the need for government to regulate business was long and difficult. Ultimately, the problem was solved when several justices retired, allowing President Roosevelt to appoint justices who believed that the "freedom to contract" had to give way to the power of government to regulate business for the greater public good. By the time the Supreme Court was made up primarily of men appointed by President Roosevelt, they were mainly concerned with upholding the power of government to regulate business, not with the question of equal rights for women. This is best illustrated by the 1948 case of *Goesaert v. Cleary*, which involved a Michigan law that made it illegal for a woman to receive a bartender's license unless she was "the wife or daughter of the male owner."[9] Felix Frankfurter wrote the opinion for the six-justice majority. He and the majority viewed the case as simply another in a long line of cases which attempted to challenge the ability of governments at all levels to regulate business. He ruled that it must be "beyond question" that Michigan had the power to prevent women from working in bars at all. Given that fact, clearly Michigan could then decide that under certain special circumstances women would be allowed to tend bar. These justices found it reasonable that the state would want to "protect" women from the bad influences of a bar; it was also reasonable for Michigan to decide that if the woman's husband or father ran the bar, he would protect her. Three justices, William O. Douglas, Frank Murphy, and Wiley B. Rutledge, saw the case differently, as one of government discrimination against women and felt that government should not be allowed to discriminate on the basis of sex in this way.

The Supreme Court began to view women as protected by the concept of equal protection in the 1970s. In 1973 the Court ruled, for example, that the U. S. military could not discriminate against women with regard to pay provisions. The case, *Frontiero v. Richardson,* involved a rule which said that a male member of the armed forces would receive a special allowance if he had a wife but that a female member of the armed forces would receive a similar allowance for her husband only if she could prove that he was actually dependent on her for his support.[10] While a majority of justices concurred that this rule had to be struck down, they could not agree on what approach to take. Should sex discrimination be viewed like race discrimination and subjected to strict scrutiny, or should some other standard be applied? The justices agreed on a result without agreeing on the reason for that result.

In 1976, Justice William J. Brennan Jr. wrote an opinion that said sex discrimination should be subjected to something less than "strict scrutiny." The case of *Craig v. Boren* involved an Oklahoma law prohibiting the sale of low-alcohol beer to men until they reached the age of twenty-one but allowing women to drink it after they reached the age of eighteen.[11] A male, Curtis Craig, sued, arguing that he was the victim of sex discrimination. Justice Brennan, writing the majority opinion, ruled that sex discrimination should be subjected to a special kind of scrutiny. He said that government could discriminate on the basis of sex if it had "important" objectives and the measures taken by government were "substantially related" to achieving those objectives. It was clear that "important" would be something less than "compelling" and that the measures would not have to be as "narrowly tailored" as that required by strict scrutiny. Justice Brennan was applying an intermediate level of scrutiny to this statute. Even so, he ruled that the Oklahoma law did not even meet this level of scrutiny. He did not find the argument that men had to be discriminated against in order to prevent drunk-driving accidents convincing.

The existence of a lower standard for sex discrimination allowed the justices to uphold government efforts to make up for past discrimination against women that probably would not have withstood strict scrutiny. There was plenty of room in this analysis for affirmative-preference programs based on sex. For example, in 1977 the Court upheld a Social Security formula for computing old-age benefits that provided more favorable benefits for women in the case of *Califano v. Webster*.[12] Women were allowed to exclude from the calculation three more low-wage years than men. This meant that if a woman and a man had similar earnings records, the woman would receive a larger Social Security retirement check. The Court felt that a long history of sex discrimination by society in general had probably caused women to earn less than men and that it was therefore acceptable for government to try and make up for past discrimination in this way. While the Court said that "archaic stereotypes" should be rejected, it also felt that the desire to "redress" society's "long-standing disparate treatment of women" was an important objective and could withstand intermediate scrutiny.

The question of the extent to which government may work to "help" women by discriminating in their favor came up again in 1982, and the recently appointed first woman to serve on the Court, Sandra Day O'Connor, cast the deciding vote. In the case of *Mississippi Women's University v. Hogan*, Joe Hogan wanted to attend nursing classes at Mississippi Women's University,[13] but the state would not allow him to attend because of his sex. Justice O'Connor, writing the opinion for the five-justice majority, rejected Mississippi's claim that it needed to operate a nursing school just for women as a kind of affirmative-action program for women. O'Connor felt that an affirmative-action program for the people who hold 98 percent of the nursing jobs made no sense. She ruled that Mississippi's all-female school was nothing more than intentional sex discrimination and that governments need an "exceedingly persuasive justification" for this kind of discrimination. She did not think helping to perpetuate the idea that women, not men, should be nurses was persuasive enough.

Four justices dissented, and Justice Lewis F. Powell wrote an impassioned dissenting opinion. He argued that single-sex schools provided special benefits to women and that it was wrong to deprive them of the option to attend such schools with government support. He argued that sex discrimination designed to "expand women's choices" should be allowed. His opinion suggested that he would have felt differently about a public university which excluded women rather than men. In his view, affirmative action for women should be upheld.

The two women who currently sit on the Court, Sandra Day O'Connor and Ruth Bader Ginsburg, have both expressed their displeasure with using a "lower standard" when reviewing sex discrimination by government. Presumably, they both realize that while such a lower standard may allow government to be beneficent to women in some instances, it could also allow government to do harm in others. The memory of the fact that in 1948 a majority of justices felt justified in "protecting" women from high-paying jobs may be uppermost in their minds. Justice O'Connor's discussion of the need for an "exceedingly persuasive justification" rather than just an "important reason" suggests that she would like to move the Court in the direction of looking at sex discrimination more strictly.

There is also an extent to which, with the passage of time, rules designed to protect or help women make less and less sense. As job opportunities increasingly open up for women, at what point does the special Social Security rule no longer make sense? The Court did not have to deal with that question in 1977, but presumably it will become an issue at some point in the future. In 1981 a majority of justices ruled in *Rostker v. Goldberg* that the federal government could discriminate in favor of women by exempting them from the military draft.[14] The majority felt that since the major purpose of the draft is to conscript soldiers to fight in combat and since women could not fight in combat under the then current federal rules, there was no sense subjecting them to the draft. By the end of 1995, America had mourned the death of one of its first female fighter pilots and watched women board combat ships for a tour of duty. At what point will it no longer make sense to "protect" women from the draft? Is there an "exceedingly persuasive justification" for excluding American women from combat, given the combat records of women serving in other armies around the world, such as that of Israel?

It is not unreasonable to believe—and the views expressed by both of the women who currently sit on the Supreme Court bears this out—that at some point in the future, sex discrimination will have to meet the same strict-scrutiny test that race discrimination is generally subjected to. When that day arrives, full equal protection will be a mixed blessing for women. Affirmative-action programs for women will have much more difficulty meeting the strict-scrutiny test.

THE CASE THAT GOT AWAY

In the spring of 1974, America expected the Supreme Court to rule on its first case involving an affirmative-action program based on race. The case of *DeFunis v. Odegaard* concerned the efforts Marco DeFunis had to expend to get into the University of Washington Law School.[15] DeFunis, a white male, was turned down for admission to the law school, while minority students with lower test scores and grades were admitted through an affirmative-action program. DeFunis sued and won his case in a Washington district court. The judge ordered the University to admit him while the case was on appeal. The Washington Supreme Court ruled against DeFunis and ordered the university to kick him out. DeFunis appealed his case to the U.S. Supreme Court, and Justice Douglas ordered the university to allow him to continue in school pending the outcome of that appeal.

William O. Douglas, the longest-serving member in Supreme Court history (1939–1975), probably harbored numerous personal feelings about this case. As a poor boy growing up in Washington State, his meteoric rise began when he was admitted to law school; at that time there was no such thing as today's standard Law School Admission Test. He probably wondered if he would have been able to pass such a test, given his personal history. He could see himself in Marco DeFunis, the white kid trying to make good. At the same time, he had voted in favor of every civil rights decision that involved expanding rights for African Americans. He had also voted to extend equal protection to women long before the majority of justices had been willing to do so.

The Court heard arguments in the case but dragged out the moment of decision. Finally, in March 1974, five justices decided that it was the better part of valor not to decide the case at all. Since Marco DeFunis was weeks away from graduation, anything the Court might rule would have no impact on him. Five justices voted to declare the case moot and refused to issue a decision. The other four justices objected to this procedure, arguing that such an important issue should be decided by the Court as quickly as possible. Justice Douglas wrote one of those dissenting opinions— perhaps the most difficult one of his career. Douglas is well known for his ability to cut to the heart of a legal matter and then write a brief decision making it clear exactly where he stood and why; that is why he is so often quoted by other justices. His language is economical and direct. In this case Douglas was unable to do that.

It is very clear in reading Douglas's opinion that he was torn between supporting efforts to help African Americans get a boost up in life and the strong desire to reject anything that might be called "reverse discrimination" against whites. His opinion has provided language that both sides of the debate could quote in the years since 1974. On the one hand, he recognized the limitations of standard admission tests to judge people who grew up outside the suburban lifestyle of the white majority. He argued that "a black applicant who pulled himself out of the ghetto" had probably demonstrated the kind of "motivation, perseverance, and ability" that would lead "a fair-minded admissions committee to conclude that he shows more promise for law study than the son of a rich alumnus who achieved better grades at Harvard." But he wondered why this logic should be limited to black and Hispanic applicants, the main beneficiaries of this particular affirmative-preference program. Wouldn't it also apply to poor Appalachian whites or second-generation Asians who grew up in Chinatown? The University of Washington Law School had a two-track admission system, one for special people (blacks, Hispanics, American Indians, and women) and one for everyone else. Douglas seemed to argue in favor of an admission system where everyone would be judged on the basis of their "individual attributes" instead of one that simply granted a "preference solely on the basis of race." At the same time, he had no clear idea how such a system could be developed given the number of applications a law school like the University of Washington had to process each year.

While Justice Douglas was unsure how to deal with his desire to help poor applicants and at the same time not support reverse discrimination, he was clear about what standard of review was necessary. Since this "affirmative-action plan" was clearly racial discrimination by government, it must be subjected to "the strictest scrutiny under the Equal Protection Clause." He felt that "the consideration of race as a measure of an applicant's qualifications normally introduces a capricious and irrelevant factor" which would ultimately lead to "invidious discrimination." He argued that once race was introduced as a deciding factor, decision makers would be "immediately embroiled in competing claims of different racial and ethnic groups that would make" the creation of "manageable standards consistent with the Equal Protection Clause" difficult if not impossible. What he wished for was a way for admissions committees to consider each applicant in a "racially neutral way." But how would that work? He accepted the idea that the Law School Admission Test was probably biased against people who came from backgrounds at variance with the middle-class culture. He also recognized that the sheer numbers of applicants made reliance on test scores the only practical way to admit students.

His opinion seemed to vacillate, as if he was trying to make up his mind and we were watching him do so. On the one hand, he wrote: "The Equal Protection Clause commands the elimination of racial barriers, not their creation in order to satisfy our theory as to how society ought to be organized." This seems clearly to reject the basic premise of affirmative-action programs that grant preferences based on race. He also said that "a segregated admissions process creates suggestions of stigma and caste no less than a segregated classroom, and in the end it may produce that result despite its contrary intentions." He concluded his opinion by writing: "So far as race is concerned, any state-sponsored preference to one race over another ... is in my view 'invidious' and violative of the Equal Protection Clause." At the same time, he ruled in favor of the University of Washington Law School and its affirmative-action plan. It is almost as if he were going to rule against the university and wrote his opinion accordingly but then changed his mind at the last minute and simply rewrote the last sentence. We will never know how he would have voted when it really counted. The next year, he suffered a stroke and resigned from the Court.

While Justice Douglas struggled with this case, there are certain themes that run through his opinion. He was unhappy with an admissions process that seemed designed to make admissions decisions easy with little regard for discovering the individual attributes of the applicants. He felt that a system which put everyone through an impersonal mathematical calculation, combining grades with admissions test scores, and came up with a number was not a very good way of deciding who should go to law school and obviously discriminated against some segments of the society. On the other hand, simply saying that minorities should be plucked out of the process and judged by a lower standard seemed a policy clearly designed to stigmatize those it purported to help. Justice Douglas had no solution except to call for a return to the process as it had been when he was admitted to law school.

Then it was a more personal process in which the individual strengths and weaknesses of each applicant were measured without the benefit, or problems, of a so-called objective admissions test.

Marco DeFunis graduated from the University of Washington Law School in 1974. The Supreme Court would not rule on the issue until 1978, when it would be forced to decide the case of Allan P. Bakke. Of course, we will never know for sure, but a majority of the justices may not have wanted the *DeFunis* case to be their first decision on affirmative action for a very simple reason: Marco DeFunis was Jewish.

7

THE SUPREME COURT
FROM BAKKE TO
ADARAND

During the 1970s many American institutions experimented with various kinds of affirmative-action plans that gave preferences based on race. In 1974 the Supreme Court refused to decide the *DeFunis* case because Marco DeFunis was about to graduate from law school. In 1978, faced with a similar case, except that the medical school in question had not been ordered to admit the "white male" pending the outcome of the case, the Court could no longer ignore what was fast becoming a fact of American life.

REGENTS OF THE
UNIVERSITY OF CALIFORNIA V. BAKKE

Allan Bakke was a white male who had applied to the new medical school at the University of California at Davis twice, in 1973 and 1974.[1] He had high scores on the medical entrance examination, good college grades, and the medical-school professors who interviewed him gave him a high ranking. Unfortunately for him, the school admitted only a hundred new students each year out of three thousand applicants, and his scores were apparently not good enough. The school also set aside sixteen places in each entering class for minorities. While the school said its special-admissions program was for the "disadvantaged," it had never admitted a disadvantaged white person. The program was intended to admit minority students, defined as black, Hispanic, Native American, and Asian, who would not otherwise be admitted. When Allan Bakke found out that minority students were being admitted with test scores substantially below his own, he filed a lawsuit.

The facts of the *Bakke* case gave Americans their first in-depth look at how a university affirmative-action program works. Part of the mythology of affirmative action had been that minorities were being admitted who had grades or test scores that were "slightly" lower when compared with white applicants. Supporters of affirmative action asked what was wrong with giving minorities who "almost made it" a "little boost." This was not exactly what had been happening at the medical school at the University of California at Davis. Allan Bakke scored in the top-ten percentile on the medical entrance exam, meaning he did better than 90 percent of those who took the exam. The average person admitted without "special consideration" scored in the top quarter of those taking the test. The average minority student admitted under the affirmative-action program scored in the bottom third. For 1973 the scores looked like this:

MEDICAL ENTRANCE EXAM
(PERCENTILE OF THOSE TAKING THE TEST)

	Verbal	Quantitative	Science	General Information
Bakke	96	94	97	72
Avg. regular	81	76	83	69
Avg. special	46	24	35	33

This was not a case of giving someone who scored in the seventies a helping hand into medical school; it gave individuals who scored in the bottom third a special ticket.

From 1971 to 1974 the medical school admitted one black, six Hispanics, and thirty-seven Asians under the regular-admissions program. The special-admissions program brought in twenty-one blacks, thirty Hispanics, and twelve Asians. While it was obvious that the Asians did not really need special consideration, it was also clear that the school would have admitted very few black and Hispanic students without the affirmative-action program.

While many thought that affirmative action meant examining minority applicants a little more closely when it came time to make admission decisions, that was not how Davis's program worked. Applications by minority students were placed in a special pile and reviewed separately from those who applied for regular admission, which meant that the sixteen affirmative-action students competed only with other minority students and were never compared with the regular students seeking admission.

When the case arrived at the California Supreme Court, these judges viewed it as simply one of race discrimination by government and applied strict scrutiny. The California Supreme Court ruled that Davis's affirmative-action program did not withstand strict scrutiny and ordered Allan Bakke admitted to the medical school. At that point, the U.S. Supreme Court agreed to hear the case.

No five justices of the Supreme Court could agree. The four more conservative justices (John Paul Stevens, Potter Stewart, William Rehnquist, and Chief Justice Warren E. Burger) refused to see it as a constitutional case. Title VI of the Civil Rights Act of 1964 outlawed racial discrimination by schools that received federal funds, and Davis had received them. Since the case was clearly one of race discrimination in violation of the law, the justices voted to order the school to admit Bakke. If Congress wanted to make an exception for affirmative action, then it could pass another statute explaining how these programs would operate, but there was no such provision in the existing statute.

The four more liberal justices (William Brennan, Byron White, Thurgood Marshall, and Harry A. Blackmun) felt that *Bakke* should be viewed as a constitutional case, but they also believed that strict scrutiny should not be used. They argued that the standard should be the one developed to deal with sex discrimination: whether or not the program served "important governmental objectives" and whether or not the steps taken were "substantially related" to the achievement of those objectives. The four justices

felt that increasing the number of minority doctors in America
was sufficiently important to justify the "remedial" use of race
when making decisions on admissions. They would have simply
affirmed that state universities had broad powers to institute
affirmative-action programs to help underrepresented racial
groups. In his opinion, Justice Brennan said that "Davis's articula-
ted purpose of remedying the effects of past societal discrimination" is important enough "to justify the use of race-conscious
admissions programs" in cases where "minority underrepresentation is substantial and chronic."

Justice Marshall, in his separate opinion, pointed out that
African Americans had been dragged to America in chains and
even after the Civil War had been subjected to all kinds of
indignities at the hands of American society. He apparently felt
that affirmative-preference programs based on race were a small
price for America to pay in return for all those decades of torment.
He did not discuss the fact that only one-third of the students who
had been admitted to the medical school at Davis under the
special-admissions program were African Americans.

Justice Blackmun, in his separate opinion, said that he hoped
the time would come as quickly as possible when affirmative-
action programs would no longer be necessary. He hoped America
could reach that stage in a decade but felt the odds of that were
slim. He did not tell us how we would know when the time had
come to end affirmative-preference programs based on race.

Justice Powell was the swing vote, and it was his decision that
really counted. He agreed with the four conservative justices that
Bakke should be admitted to the medical school, so Bakke got his
chance to be a doctor. At the same time, he did not agree with the
four conservative justices that this case raised only issues of
statutory interpretation. The Equal Protection Clause of the
Fourteenth Amendment had to be considered because Davis was a
state university and the case obviously involved race discrimination by the state. Having said that, he was not willing to go along
with the liberal justices and use some lower standard of analysis in
order to justify so-called remedial discrimination. He said that
"equal protection cannot mean one thing when applied to one

individual and something else when applied to a person of another color."

Justice Powell ruled that strict scrutiny must be applied to a case of race discrimination by the government even if the discrimination was in the form of affirmative action. He said that any affirmative-preference program was likely to "reinforce common stereotypes" about the inability of minorities to compete on their own merits, which would not be a desirable result. He also quoted Justice Douglas's opinion in the *DeFunis* case in which Douglas had argued that such a program based on race alone might "exacerbate racial and ethnic antagonisms rather than alleviate them."

Justice Powell then looked at the university's arguments to see if any of them were "compelling" enough to meet the strict-scrutiny test. The university had offered four reasons to justify the affirmative-action plan: First, it wanted to redress the historical absence of some minority groups from the medical profession; second, it wanted to make up for past societal discrimination; third, it hoped that many of the minority doctors would decide to practice in poor neighborhoods and make up for a lack of medical care in such areas; and fourth, it wanted to "obtain the educational benefits that flow from an ethnically diverse student body." Powell rejected the first three reasons as not compelling enough. While he felt that past discrimination on the part of a particular governmental unit could justify reverse discrimination, Davis was a new medical school, and it had no record of past discrimination. Trying to correct societal discrimination or hoping that minority students might decide to practice in poor neighborhoods was not "compelling" enough to justify race discrimination.

The fourth reason was another story. The Supreme Court had interpreted the First Amendment to provide some measure of protection for universities in the name of academic freedom. Justice Powell felt that such academic freedom should include the right to select students. He agreed that different students bring diverse backgrounds to the campus and that the educational experience could be enriched for everyone if such students were admitted.

At the same time, Powell rejected the use of a special two-track admissions system. He ruled that in considering the individual merits of particular students, public universities could consider the person's race as a "plus" in trying to achieve diversity. He pointed to the admissions program at Harvard University as a model for others to follow. At Harvard a variety of factors are considered, from the geographic area in which the person grew up to the person's race, in order to achieve a diverse student body. Justice Powell described in great detail the kind of admissions program he felt would meet the dictates of the Constitution. While race could be considered, it would have to be just one of many factors taken into consideration, along with "exceptional personal talents, unique work or service experience, leadership potential, maturity, demonstrated compassion, a history of overcoming disadvantage, ability to communicate with the poor, and other qualifications deemed important."

There is a sense of unreality in Justice Powell's decision. He seemed to forget that the faculty of the University of California at Davis medical school had three thousand applicants and could not possibly give every one of them personal attention. He was apparently trying to mandate the kind of review Justice Douglas called for in his *DeFunis* opinion without regard for the realities of modern university admissions.

Of eight justices, only one, Justice Powell, applied the strict-scrutiny test in the *Bakke* case, and he alone ruled that the desire of a public university to achieve "diversity" in its student body could justify taking race into consideration when making admissions decisions. A majority of justices would never agree that the desire to achieve diversity in any social institution met the strict scrutiny test.

Justice Brennan, writing for the four more liberal justices, argued that a different test should be used to judge affirmative-action programs and that under this "lower standard" the desire to overcome past "societal discrimination" was "sufficiently important" to meet this test. He would not get a fifth vote for that proposition in *Bakke* or in any subsequent case.

Over the next two decades this decision would stand as the

only word from the Supreme Court on the issue of whether or not state universities could take race into consideration when making admissions decisions. While the opinion of Justice Powell became the law of the land on this subject, the *Bakke* decision would have no precedential impact on a future Supreme Court that wanted to reexamine the issue because no five justices could agree on a single opinion.

STEELWORKERS V. WEBER

The next year, 1979, the Supreme Court found an affirmative-action plan that a majority of justices could accept.[2] The case involved affirmative action by a private employer rather than government, so there was no question of having to interpret the Constitution or to apply strict scrutiny. The question was: Did the Civil Rights Act of 1964 allow private employers to engage in voluntary affirmative action that gave a preference to people because of their race? A majority of the justices ruled that it did.

In 1974, Kaiser Aluminum and Chemical Corporation and its union, faced with the realization that blacks held very few skilled positions in its southern plants, agreed that half of all the training positions for skilled jobs would be reserved for black employees until their numbers in skilled positions matched the percentage of blacks in the local labor force. Prior to 1974, although blacks made up 39 percent of the local labor force, less than 2 percent of the skilled jobs in Kaiser's southern plants were held by blacks. Seniority and race would be the criteria for deciding which current unskilled workers would be chosen for the training programs. A white man, Brian Weber, sued when a training position was given to a black man with less seniority.

The federal district court and the appeals court ruled that this kind of open and obvious race discrimination clearly violated Title VII of the Civil Rights Act of 1964. President Carter's Justice Department argued that private employers should be allowed to set up a voluntary affirmative-action program when it could be seen as a "reasonable response to an arguable violation of Title VII." It was obvious to everyone that thousands of employers in the South would have to do something to make up for past racial discrimination. If the Supreme Court forced them all to go through some kind of lawsuit, it would be very expensive and time consuming not only for the businesses involved but for the federal government.

Justice Brennan, writing the opinion for the five-justice majority (Stewart, White, Marshall, and Blackmun), refused to restrict voluntary affirmative-action plans in this way. He pointed out that Section 703(j) of the Civil Rights Act says that nothing in the law "required" preferential treatment. He argued that if Congress had wanted to outlaw affirmative action, it could have done so by saying that the law did not "require or permit" preferential treatment. Because it did not, he concluded that Congress had no intention of outlawing all voluntary affirmative-action programs by private employers. Justice Brennan said that Kaiser's voluntary affirmative-action plan was designed to "break down old patterns of racial segregation." The plan did not "unnecessarily trammel the interests of the white employees"—half of the training positions would still go to them—and it did not require that they be discharged. He also pointed out that it was a temporary plan and would end when the percentage reached what might have been expected had there been no past discrimination by society in general or by Kaiser in particular.

Justice Blackmun wrote a concurring opinion pointing out that the majority of justices had decided to allow voluntary affirmative-action plans by private employers in order to integrate "traditionally segregated job categories" if there was evidence of a "societal history of purposeful exclusion" of groups in that job category. He felt that doing so would allow more affirmative action than the Justice Department's suggested test, which was that it be a "reasonable response to an arguable violation" of the civil rights laws. He said that the justices decided not to get into the question of what was or was not an "arguable violation" for fear that most employers would not want to subject themselves to possible legal liability by admitting that they had probably violated the civil rights laws in the past.

Justice Blackmun tried to make it clear what he and the other justices who voted in favor of this voluntary affirmative-action plan by a private employer were saying: that when a "traditionally segregated job category" exists because of "a societal history of purposeful exclusion" of a particular group from that job category, a private employer may institute an affirmative-action plan to make up for that past discrimination by society in general. In other words, "societal discrimination" could be used to justify affirmative-preference programs by private employers based on race without violating Title VII, but only for traditionally segregated job categories. It was not clear who would decide which job categories had been traditionally segregated.

Both Justice Brennan and Justice Blackmun pointed out that Congress could amend the law if it was not happy with the Court's interpretation. Presumably they both knew that efforts to limit affirmative action had been rejected when the Civil Rights Act of 1972 was being considered and that Congress was not going to write a general statute dealing with the issue of affirmative action.

Chief Justice Burger wrote a dissenting opinion for the four more conservative justices. He stated that the Civil Rights Act of 1964 specifically outlawed discrimination in a "training program" and that this affirmative-action program was nothing more, or less, than racial discrimination in a training program.

What every justice on the Court presumably knew but was not willing to openly discuss was that Section 703(j) of the 1964 Civil Rights Act, the section Justice Brennan used to justify his interpretation of the law, had been added to the statute only to placate southern politicians, such as Sen. James O. Eastland from Mississippi, who would not have voted for the act without it, and that its express purpose was to prevent the creation of affirmative-action plans. At least that had been the purpose that had been "expressed" to those southern politicians. Justice Brennan's use of Section 703(j) to justify voluntary affirmative-action plans was one of the great acts of judicial legerdemain in Supreme Court history.

FULLILOVE V. KLUTZNICK

In 1980 the Court finally found an affirmative-action plan that even Chief Justice Burger could support.[3] Congress had passed the

Public Works Employment Act in 1977, a law which required that 10 percent of federal funds granted to state and local governments for public works projects be used to procure goods and services from minority-owned businesses. The act defined minority as "Negroes, Spanish-speaking, Orientals, Indians, Eskimos, and Aleuts." The act allowed for the waiver of this requirement if no suitable minority firms could be found. Congress stated that the purpose of the act was to provide access to public contracting opportunities to firms that had been "impaired by the effects of prior discrimination."

Chief Justice Burger, joined by Justice White, wrote the opinion for the Court. He refused to discuss whether strict scrutiny should be applied or whether Congress had a compelling reason to use racial preference in this case. He pointed out that Congress had been given special powers in the Fourteenth Amendment to "enforce by appropriate legislation" the provisions of the amendment. He felt that this authorized Congress to require states spending federal money to create a set-aside program for minority contractors.

Justice Powell did want to talk about standards. In a concurring opinion, he said that strict scrutiny should apply to the federal government as well as state and local government and that the desire to "eradicate continuing effects of past discrimination" was a compelling enough reason to introduce a federal affirmative-action plan.

Justice Marshall, joined by Justices Brennan and Blackmun, argued that affirmative action should not be subjected to strict scrutiny. He felt that government should only be required to have an "important" reason to engage in affirmative action; the desire to remedy the effects of past societal discrimination was important enough.

The three dissenting justices—Stewart, Rehnquist, and Stevens—argued that strict scrutiny should be applied even if the federal government is involved and that the desire to overcome some general discrimination by society was not a good enough reason. Justice Stewart argued that this decision was wrong "for the same reason *Plessy v. Ferguson* was wrong." He went on to say that "because of the Court's decision today, our statute books will once again have to contain laws that reflect the odious practice of delineating the qualities that make one person a Negro and make another a white."

Justice Stevens asked how Congress came up with the list of particular minority groups entitled to special treatment. He could not see how such a vague list could ever meet the test of strict scrutiny. He felt that since "racial characteristics so seldom provide a relevant basis for disparate treatment" and "are potentially so harmful to the entire body politic, it is especially important that the reasons for any such classification be clearly identified and unquestionably legitimate." He could not find a clear identification of the reasons for the classification in this statute. He referred to Justice Marshall's opinion in *Bakke* in which he had chronicled the history of harm done to Negroes in America and pointed out that "the history of discrimination against black citizens in America cannot justify a grant of privileges to Eskimos or Indians." He also pointed out that while African Americans had been brought to America in chains, the "Spanish-speaking" had come voluntarily, "frequently without invitation," and that the Indians, the Eskimos, and the Aleuts "had an opportunity to exploit America's resources before the ancestors of most American citizens arrived." Stevens argued that this particular kind of affirmative-action plan—a program that helps only those with enough money to start a business—is "perverse" because "those who are the most disadvantaged within each class are the least likely to receive any benefit from the special privilege." He felt that providing a benefit to "a favored few" was a poor way to compensate "for an injury shared by many." He wondered if racial preferences would be written into law simply because a particular group had "the political strength" to negotiate "a piece of the action."

Turning to the details of this particular set-aside program, Justice Stevens imagined that there are five types of minority-owned firms: first, firms that are able to get contracts without special help; second, firms that never tried to get a government contract; third, firms that will be formed simply to take advantage of the special program; fourth, firms that failed to get government contracts in the past for reasons other than race discrimination; and fifth, firms that have actually been the victims of race discrimination. Stevens argued that this set-aside program was not "narrowly tailored" to deal with the stated problem because it did not attempt to find out which firms fit into the fifth category. He ended his opinion by saying:

> A statute of this kind inevitably is perceived by many as resting on an assumption that those who are granted this special preference are less qualified in some respect that is identified purely by their race. Because that perception— especially when fostered by the Congress of the United States—can only exacerbate rather than reduce racial prejudice, it will delay the time when race will become a truly irrelevant, or at least insignificant, factor.

Justice Stevens's dissenting opinion in this case is very important because it would echo in the minds of all the justices in the years that followed.

From the point of view of the general public, the Supreme Court had handed down three decisions on affirmative action in three years, and affirmative action had won each time. The news media did not dwell on questions of whether or not "strict scrutiny" had been applied or whether or not this or that program met the test.

The *Fullilove* decision appeared to give the federal government a blank check to create affirmative-action plans. While *Weber* allowed private employers to create voluntary affirmative-action programs only if certain circumstances existed, few bothered to ask if their particular affirmative-action plan met the standards set out in *Weber*. Instead, most created their plan at the insistence of the OFCC and did not view what they were doing as voluntary. The same could be said for most affirmative-action plans instituted by state and local governments. Behind most programs was some agency of the federal government demanding a plan, complete with goals, timetables, and measurable results.

Three justices—Brennan, Marshall, and Blackmun—obviously felt that the other branches of the federal government were not willing to do what they should to encourage affirmative action. They believed that it would be best for America to move as fast and as far as it could toward integration using affirmative-action plans. Because of this belief, they argued that strict scrutiny should not be used in cases of "positive" race discrimination by federal, state, and local governments. Rather, an easier test should be applied, one that most affirmative-action plans could meet. What they did not want to discuss was that from the point of view of those whites who were affected by such plans, positive race discrimination looked a lot like negative race discrimination. The Court had ruled in the past that everyone, white and black, was entitled to equal protection under the law. How could this be reconciled with the obvious fact that when preferences were given to minorities, it meant that whites who met the "usual" criteria were not admitted into medical school, given a high-paying job, or awarded a lucrative government contract. Because of such obvious contradictions, the three justices could never get two other votes for the concept that some kind of "lower" standard should be used in cases involving government affirmative-action plans.

In the *Fullilove* case Chief Justice Burger and Justice White were willing to say only that the federal government was somehow different and did not have to meet the same standard that applied to state and local government, which was a departure from past decisions that had held that "equal" meant just that in all cases. None of the justices wanted to discuss the potential problems that might flow from a definition of equality that would be different depending on the level of government involved.

FIREFIGHTERS V. STOTTS

In 1984 the Court decided the *Stotts* case.[4] The city of Memphis had been sued over race discrimination in its fire department. To settle the case, the city instituted an affirmative-action plan for blacks. Then the city got into financial trouble and had to lay off some of its firefighters. If the city had followed the usual procedure, it would have laid off the most recently hired, which would have included many of the newly hired black firefighters. The federal district judge ordered the city not to follow the usual procedure but instead to lay off whites with more seniority. The Supreme Court overruled the decision.

Justice White wrote the opinion for the six-justice majority. He pointed out that the Civil Rights Act of 1964 specifically authorized the use of seniority when making personnel decisions. He argued that laying off white employees because of their race was very different from not hiring them in the first place. After this decision, it would never be legal to fire white workers in order to make room for minorities or women under an affirmative-action plan.

WYGANT V. JACKSON BOARD OF EDUCATION

In 1986 the Court was faced with a Michigan school board that had signed a contract with the teachers union agreeing to lay off more senior white teachers in order to keep minority teachers employed.[5] Both the federal district judge and the Sixth Circuit Court agreed that the contract was legal and constitutional. The reason for the special agreement was to overcome "societal discrimination" and to retain as many minority teachers as possible to provide role models for minority students.

The Supreme Court rejected both of these justifications for affirmative action. Justice Powell wrote the opinion for himself and three other justices (Rehnquist, O'Connor, and Chief Justice Burger). He said that this was race discrimination by state and local government and therefore strict scrutiny had to be applied. He ruled that attempting to overcome societal discrimination and providing role models for minority students were not compelling enough reasons to justify race discrimination. If the role-model theory were enough to justify race discrimination, then as the racial makeup of the student body changed each year, teachers would have to be hired or fired depending on their race in order to get the right racial mix.

Justice O'Connor wrote a concurring opinion pointing out that she agreed with the use of strict scrutiny whenever affirmative action by government was involved and that in her opinion the plan clearly did not stand up to strict scrutiny.

Justice White wrote a concurring opinion in which he re-emphasized what he had said in *Stotts*, that being laid off was too great a burden on white employees. He did not discuss whether or not he was applying strict scrutiny. He simply said that the plan was clearly a violation of the Equal Protection Clause.

Justices Marshall, Brennan, and Blackmun dissented. They were joined by Justice Stevens, which was a surprise, for he had voted against affirmative action in the past. In this case he voted for it because he believed that providing a role model for school-children was a good enough reason to justify race-based hiring and firing policies by public school districts. A majority of the justices would never agree with this position.

In this case, Justice White seemed to be moving from pro–affirmative action to anti–affirmative action, while Justice Stevens was moving in the opposite direction. Because they both refused to sign on to one of the two major decisions in the case, lawyers and judges in America were left with very little concrete guidance from the Supreme Court.

SHEET METAL WORKERS V. EEOC

However, in 1986 the Court did provide guidance to federal judges faced with cases of proven, intentional race discrimination.[6] The case involved the New York City local of the Sheet Metal Workers Union, which was found to have violated the Civil Rights Act in 1975. Over the years the federal judge had tried a variety of ways to bring the union into compliance with the law, but nothing seemed to work. Finally, the union was ordered to bring in nonwhite members until 29 percent of the membership was nonwhite. Justice Brennan wrote an opinion, joined by Justices Marshall, Blackmun, and Stevens, approving of the court-ordered affirmative-action plan. He ruled that once the judge found intentional race discrimination, he had broad powers to remedy the problem.

Justice Powell wrote a concurring opinion in which he spelled out what he liked about the judge's affirmative-action plan. The plan was temporary, it could be waived by the judge if enough qualified nonwhites could not be found, and it did not require any whites to lose their jobs. Justice O'Connor also wrote a concurring opinion in which she approved of the fact that the judge had given the union a "goal" rather than a "quota."

Justice White, who had voted with Brennan and Marshall in the *Bakke* and *Weber* cases, dissented. He felt that an affirmative action plan that gave jobs or union membership to those who had not actually been discriminated against in the past went too far. Rehnquist and Burger agreed with White. In their opinion, only the actual victims of past discrimination should be allowed to benefit from an affirmative-action plan.

Some commentators saw the decision to allow court-ordered affirmative action for individuals who were not the proven victims of past discrimination as a major departure from general principles of law. The justices who approved of it did not see it this way. Everyone knew that many minorities had never even tried to join this union because that would have been a waste of time, given its reputation in the community for race discrimination. It was impossible to actually determine who "might" have tried to join the union if the union had not been known to racially discriminate. The only way to attempt to find such people was to announce that the union was now required to accept black members and depend on those who had been the victims of race discrimination by this labor union to show up and ask for membership.

UNITED STATES V. PARADISE

By February 1987, Justice Rehnquist had been elevated to chief justice and Justice Antonin Scalia had been appointed to the Court by President Reagan.[7] Neither justice would ever find an affirmative-action plan he could support. The *Paradise* case was fairly straightforward; the federal district judge in Alabama had tried everything to get the state of Alabama to integrate the state police. When nothing worked, he ordered the state to make sure that half of all the new recruits were black until 25 percent of the force was black. A few years later, it had become painfully clear that very few of the new black officers had been promoted to corporal, so the judge ordered the state to promote one black officer for each white officer promoted until 25 percent of the corporals were black.

Justice Brennan, joined by Marshall, Blackmun, and Powell, wrote the opinion. He found the court-ordered affirmative-action plan acceptable because the judge had found the state guilty of intentional race discrimination. Justice Powell agreed. He approved of this judge's order for the same reasons he had liked that of the judge in the *Sheet Metal Workers* case.

Justice Stevens also agreed, providing the fifth vote in favor of the plan. In his opinion, the case was one of "egregious violation" of both the law and the constitution; there was no need to discuss whether or not the judge's order met the requirements of strict scrutiny.

Chief Justice Rehnquist, along with Justices White and Scalia, opposed this kind of court order. They were joined by Justice O'Connor, who wrote a dissenting opinion. She felt that strict scrutiny should be applied to a judge's order, since it is a kind of government action; she did not feel that the judge's order met the requirements of strict scrutiny. She did not believe that a quota should be ordered in this way. While overcoming proven past race discrimination was certainly a compelling reason to use some kind of affirmative-action plan, this plan was not "narrowly tailored" enough in her opinion. It was not clear from the dissenting opinions what the justices thought a federal judge should do when faced with a case like the Alabama state police.

JOHNSON V. SANTA CLARA COUNTY

The *Johnson* decision, handed down in March 1987, marked the last time six justices would be able to concur in an affirmative-action case.[8] The case was unique in many ways. First of all, while it involved a case of affirmative action by government, the plaintiff's attorney had not raised the issue of whether or not the plan violated the constitutional concept of equal protection. Because of this, Justice Brennan, who wrote the opinion for the five-justice majority, refused to discuss whether or not the plan would have met the test of strict scrutiny.

The case involved the efforts of Santa Clara County, California, to hire more women in areas where few women had ever been hired. In one job category, "Skilled Craft," there were 238 positions and no women employees. When an opening occurred, the two top candidates for the job were Paul Johnson and Diane Joyce. A panel of administrators reviewed the records, interviewed the top candidates, and gave each one a score based on the panel's opinion of their ability to do a good job. The panel gave Paul Johnson, a white man, a score of 75 and Diane Joyce, a white woman, a score of 73. The administrator responsible for making the final decision then hired Diane Joyce as part of the county's affirmative-action plan. The county said it was trying to redress a "gross underrepresentation" of women in a "traditionally segregated job category."

Justice Brennan viewed the case as very similar to *Weber*. In that decision the Court had ruled that employers did not violate Title VII if they instituted a voluntary affirmative-action plan in order to eliminate "traditional patterns" of racial segregation. Here the county was simply trying to correct a "significant underrepresentation" of women in a "traditionally segregated job classification." Justice Brennan pointed out that the county had not set up a quota, but merely goals to guide future hiring decisions.

Justice O'Connor was the sixth vote in favor of Diane Joyce. However, she wanted to analyze the case under the concept of equal protection. O'Connor argued that when an imbalance is so great, it should be seen as evidence of past intentional discrimination by the particular government employer. Because in her mind it was a case of using affirmative action to overcome past intentional discrimination, it met the strict-scrutiny test. Justice O'Connor believed that trying to overcome past discrimination by society in general was not compelling but overcoming it by the agency in question *was*. She also felt that the affirmative-action plan met the strict-scrutiny test because it did not set up quotas. Sex was simply a "plus" to be considered when hiring or promoting qualified candidates.

Chief Justice Rehnquist and Justices Scalia and White dissented. The dissents of Rehnquist and Scalia were certainly expected, but White's was a surprise. He had voted with the majority in favor of voluntary affirmative action in the *Weber* case. In his dissenting opinion, White argued that *Weber* should be overruled. He said that when he voted with the majority in that case he thought he was allowing voluntary affirmative-action plans only when it was clear that the employer had engaged in past discrimination. He did not feel that Santa Clara County fell in to that category, and he was disappointed with what he felt was a "perversion of Title VII." Apparently, Justice White had not been paying attention to what went on in the *Weber* case. The Carter Justice Department had suggested that the Court allow voluntary affirmative action only when there was an "arguable violation of Title VII." Justice White could have refused to sign Justice Brennan's decision and instead written one of his own. Then his word would have been law, just as Justice Powell's was in the *Bakke* case. Of course, even Supreme Court justices are not allowed to go back and do things over. He was as stuck with the clear implications of the *Weber* decision as everyone else.

CITY OF RICHMOND V. CROSON

The *Croson* case involved the efforts of Richmond, Virginia, to set aside 30 percent of the city's contracts for minority-owned businesses.[9] Richmond used the same definition of minority that Congress had used in the Public Works Employment Act of 1977. That meant that "blacks, Spanish-speaking, Orientals, Indians, Eskimos, and Aleuts" were entitled to take advantage of the special program.

Justice O'Connor, writing the opinion for the majority, ruled that because *Croson* was a case of intentional race discrimination by state and local government, it must be subjected to strict scrutiny. In this case there was no geographic limit. Eskimos, who had never set foot in Virginia and who could not possibly have been the victims of discrimination in Richmond, could take advantage of the plan even though the stated reason for the plan was to remedy past discrimination by Richmond's construction industry. O'Connor pointed out that simply calling a plan "remedial" did not make it so. The city had no evidence concerning how much discrimination had taken place in the past, and it certainly had none concerning the extent to which Eskimos had been the victims of discrimination. Only the desire to remedy "real" past discrimination could stand up to strict scrutiny, and the Richmond plan did not qualify. Moreover, there was no evidence as to why the city decided on 30 percent as a set-aside. In other words, it was not a "narrowly tailored" plan to overcome proven past racial discrimination.

Justice Stevens was the sixth vote to strike down the Richmond plan. He could not see how the city could justify a plan that granted special privileges to groups that had never tried to do business in the city.

In his concurring opinion, Justice Scalia quoted from Justice Douglas's opinion in the *DeFunis* case, suggesting that cities grant preferences to "new" or "small" businesses instead of to those owned by preferred racial groups. He argued that such a program would accomplish many of the stated objectives without the stigma of racial discrimination.

Justices Brennan, Marshall, and Blackmun dissented. Justice Blackmun expressed his disbelief that the Supreme Court would prevent the city of Richmond, the former capital of the Confederate States of America, from instituting an affirmative-action plan. He was not bothered by the fact that there was no evidence that most of the groups listed in the plan had ever been discriminated against by anyone in Richmond, Virginia.

Although commentators have argued that the law of affirmative action took a sharp turn to the right with the Court's decision in *Croson*, that is not really the case. In 1986, with the decision in *Wygant*, four justices had said that state and local government affirmative-action programs should have to stand up to strict scrutiny. Justice White's refusal to join in the reasoning of the opinion prevented it from being a clear majority. Just as the plan to lay off white teachers in *Wygant* did not stand up to the strict scrutiny of four justices, the plan to set aside city contracts for a long list of preferred groups did not stand up to the strict scrutiny of five justices in *Croson*. It was important, however, that for the first time a clear majority of five justices applied the strict-scrutiny test to a state or local government affirmative-action plan and found it wanting.

METRO BROADCASTING INC. V. FCC

The 1990 decision in *Metro Broadcasting* was against the trend in this area.[10] While the Court was moving to apply strict scrutiny to state and local government affirmative-action plans and striking them down because they did not meet the test, *Metro Broadcasting* was a different matter. The case involved two minority-preference policies of the FCC. One policy considered race a plus in any application for a new broadcast license; the other allowed a current license holder who was under investigation for violations to avoid a hearing and possible sanctions by selling the license to a minority-owned enterprise. While these policies were created by the FCC rather than mandated by a specific act of Congress, Justice Brennan pointed out that when the FCC had announced that it intended to review them in 1987, the 1988 appropriations bill specifically prohibited the FCC from spending any money to examine or change its minority-preference policies. Apparently he felt that such an action by Congress gave the FCC policies some kind of legitimacy that they would not otherwise have had.

In this case the Court ruled, as it had in *Fullilove*, that the federal government did not have to meet the same standard that applied to state and local government. While the FCC policies did not meet the strict-scrutiny test, they certainly did serve an "important" government objective—the desire to increase broadcast diversity. In Justice Brennan's opinion, that objective was sufficient.

Justice O'Connor, in her dissenting opinion, strongly objected to the idea that something less than strict scrutiny should be applied to the actions of the federal government. She did not believe that one set of rules should apply to racial discrimination by the states and another to racial discrimination by the federal government. She argued that only the need to remedy past discrimination was compelling enough to justify race discrimination by government at any level. She did not believe that the desire to further something as "amorphous and insubstantial" as "broadcast diversity" should be allowed to justify racial discrimination by government.

Justice Anthony Kennedy, who joined the Court in 1988, also wrote a dissenting opinion. He referred to the Court's decision in *Plessy v. Ferguson*, in which a majority of the justices felt that "separate but equal" was a reasonable policy. He did not think the Court should go from "separate but equal" to "unequal but benign."

It was clear from these dissenting opinions that four justices were ready to reexamine the 1980 *Fullilove* decision, which had given the federal government great latitude to grant racial preferences as long as they were part of some kind of affirmative-action plan. The Court finally got a chance to reconsider the question in 1995.

Adarand Constructors v. Pena

The 1995 *Adarand* case involved the command of federal statutes to set aside 10 percent of public works contracts for minorities.[11] Adarand lost a job to a Hispanic-owned construction company even though he had been the low bidder. The general contractor who awarded the subcontract to the Hispanic-owned company received a bonus of $10,000 from the federal government because it used the minority-owned company. Adarand sued for race discrimination. The case involved provisions of the Surface Transportation and Uniform Relocation Assistance Act of 1987, which set aside 10 percent of the money for small businesses owned and controlled by "socially and economically disadvantaged" individuals. Women and minorities are presumed to be disadvantaged under the regulations.

In what was a major shift for the Court, the five-justice majority ruled that even affirmative-action plans created by the federal government must meet the strict-scrutiny test. Writing for the majority, Justice O'Connor said that there must be a "compelling purpose" served and the plan must be "narrowly tailored" to meet that compelling purpose. This decision overturned *Fullilove* and *Metro Broadcasting*, both of which stood for the proposition that the federal government did not have to meet the strict-scrutiny test when creating affirmative-action programs. O'Connor stated that past Court decisions established three propositions concerning race-based programs: (1) skepticism— "preferences based on racial or ethnic criteria must necessarily receive a most searching examination"; (2) consistency—the standard of review should not depend on the particular race of the people either "burdened or benefited" by the plan; and (3) congruence—equal-protection analysis should be the same whether a state or the federal government is involved. She then concluded that these three propositions required the Court to subject the affirmative-action programs of the federal government to strict scrutiny.

Both Justice Scalia and Justice Thomas wrote concurring opinions in which they pointed out that they could not imagine a situation in which race-based discrimination, even when called affirmative action, could withstand their personal version of strict scrutiny. Justice Scalia said, "Government can never have a compelling interest in discriminating on the basis of race." Justice Thomas argued that "so-called benign discrimination teaches many that because of chronic and apparently immutable handicaps, minorities cannot compete with them without their patronizing indulgence." Justice Thomas rejected the "paternalism" that he felt was "at the heart of this program" and all the negative images that go with that paternalism. He said "racial paternalism and its unintended consequences can be as poisonous and pernicious as any other form of discrimination." He did not think there should be a "racial paternalism exception to the principle of equal protection."

Justices Stevens, Ginsburg, David Souter, and Stephen Breyer

dissented. Justice Stevens's opinion is the most interesting because
he dissented from the majority decision in *Fullilove*, which had
upheld the idea that the federal government did not have to meet
the strict scrutiny standard. In that dissent he had argued that the
federal government should be subjected to strict scrutiny and that
the set-aside program could not possibly meet this standard. In his
dissent in the *Adarand* case, Justice Stevens argued that there is a
fundamental difference between racial discrimination designed to
"perpetuate a caste system" and one that seeks to "eradicate racial
subordination." In other words, Justice Stevens had changed his
mind between *Fullilove* and *Adarand*.

The Clinton administration may have been at least partly
responsible for the Court's decision in *Adarand*. During the spring
of 1995, in a highly publicized case involving a laid-off public-
school teacher, the Clinton administration urged the federal
circuit court to rule in favor of the school district, which chose to
lay off the white teacher rather than the black teacher in order to
maintain racial diversity.[12] The Clinton administration argued that
school districts should be free to do whatever it takes to "ensure
racial diversity in the workplace." By urging the court to endorse
"diversity" in the workplace rather than the goal of overcoming
past discrimination, the Clinton administration was apparently
trying to push the law of affirmative action to a new level. In the
Spring 1995 issue of the *Employee Relations Law Journal*,
William Kilberg suggested that this pressure might backfire.[13] He
wrote:

> The argument of Justice Scalia has been that once race and
> gender bias are permitted other than as specific remedies
> for identified victims of proven discrimination, there
> forms a slippery slope that leads inexorably to the use of
> quotas for all employment activity. Title VII would be-
> come a law favoring discrimination rather than banning it.
> Employers for the most part have belittled this risk,
> believing that race or gender "sensitivity" in employment
> decisions need not become transformed in this way. The
> Clinton administration seems determined to prove Justice
> Scalia right. Its efforts, ostensibly on behalf of affirmative

action, may well result in the demise of affirmative action
as a weapon in the battle for nondiscrimination.

What William Kilberg feared has indeed come to pass. The
Clinton administration convinced the Supreme Court that the
time to end affirmative-preference programs was in 1995, before
the Clinton administration could do any more harm.

The importance of the *Adarand* decision cannot be overstated.
For two decades both government entities and private companies
had not worried about what the Supreme Court ruled in the area
of affirmative action because they could point to a rule of the
federal government which forced them to create their particular
affirmative-action plan. With the decision in *Adarand*, the Supreme Court overturned the vast majority of those federal affirmative-action programs. State and local governments and private
employers will find that most of their affirmative-action plans are
no longer legal.

For two decades the Supreme Court had tried to come up with
a logical and consistent way to approve of government affirmative-
preference programs based on race. It toyed with the idea that the
federal government could be allowed to do what state and local
governments could not do without violating the concept of equal
protection under the law. It also explored the idea of using one test
for "good" racial discrimination and another for "bad" racial
discrimination. Both efforts were doomed to failure. Equal means
equal, and race discrimination is race discrimination. Different
tests for different "kinds" of race discrimination, or for different
levels of government, meant abandoning the ideal of equality
written into the Constitution. Ultimately, the Court was not
willing to do that. As of June 1995 the Court had finally made
clear what had been anything but clear before: Racial discrimination by government, regardless of the level of government or the
stated reason for the discrimination, was subject to strict scrutiny.
Racial discrimination by others, at the command of government,
would also be subject to strict scrutiny. Would most affirmative-
preference programs created by federal, state, and local governments be able to stand up to strict scrutiny?

8

THE LAW AFTER ADARAND

In the *Adarand* case the Supreme Court ruled that all government affirmative-action plans based on race must pass the strict scrutiny test. The Court also made it clear what it takes to survive that test. First, the plans must be temporary, with a definite end point in sight. Second, the purpose of the plan must be to remedy past discrimination against a specific ethnic group either by a particular governmental entity or by people inside the entity's jurisdiction. The desire to achieve diversity, with the possible exception of admissions to state universities, is not a compelling reason. The same is true of the desire to correct for societal discrimination or to create role models. Third, the plans must be narrowly tailored to achieve a specific result. Vague rules that seem to have been pulled out of a hat will not meet the test of strict scrutiny.

THE FEDERAL GOVERNMENT

Are any of the 162 racial-preference programs of the federal government going to meet the strict-scrutiny test? The clear answer is *no*. On June 28, 1995, the Clinton Justice Department sent a thirty-seven-page memorandum to all the federal agencies calling on them to examine their racial-preference programs to see if these programs comply with strict scrutiny. The memorandum, written by Asst. Atty. Gen. Walter Dellinger, suggested that programs created without clear guidelines from Congress would probably not meet strict scrutiny. The vast majority of racial-preference programs in the federal government do not have clear guidelines from Congress. He wrote that plans created to bring about some kind of diversity or to end societal discrimination rather than to remedy past discrimination against specific ethnic groups would not qualify. Most federal affirmative-preference programs were created to bring about diversity or to end societal discrimination, not to address specific discrimination problems. He also suggested that plans set up without any in-depth study of a particular problem would not meet the strict-scrutiny test. Most federal affirmative-preference programs were created without any in-depth study of a particular problem. He also pointed out that plans that set aside a particular percentage of something for the favored minority groups would not meet the test because that would amount to quotas rather than goals. In Dellinger's opinion, strict quotas are not going to meet the strict-scrutiny test.

What the memorandum did not state is the obvious: None of the federal government's racial-preference programs are going to meet the strict-scrutiny test. That is true of the programs mandated by Congress and of those that were simply created out of thin air by the bureaucracy. We have only to look at the dissenting opinion by Justice Stevens in the *Fullilove* case to understand why the 10 percent set-aside program for public works projects created by Congress is not going to withstand strict scrutiny. There is nothing to explain how Congress came up with the list of favored ethnic groups—Negroes, Spanish-speaking, Orientals, Indians, Eskimos, and Aleuts. There was no exhaustive study of the problem by Congress or anyone else. As Justice Stevens suggested, groups seem to appear on the list because of their political clout rather than because they have been the proven victims of particular discriminatory actions. Also, there is nothing to explain how Congress came up with the figure of 10 percent. Why not 15, 20, or 30 percent? Again, as Justice Stevens noted, the set-aside program was clearly not narrowly tailored to achieve a remedial goal.

When we think of the federal government's affirmative-preference programs, the public works set-aside program certainly comes to mind, but it represents just the tip of the iceberg. The most important federal affirmative-action program is run by the OFCC. The regulations from that office have caused hundreds of thousands of private businesses to institute goals and timetables to bring more women and minorities into every level of their workforce. These regulations are not going to stand up to strict scrutiny any more than those which implement the contract set-aside programs. The world's largest system of quotas will have to be dismantled by the same OFCC that created them in the first place.

Dozens of quota programs designed to promote minorities in federal agencies will also not stand up to strict scrutiny. In a 1991 issue of the *Military Law Review,* Capt. Donovan Bigelow examined the army's current method of promoting people to see if it could withstand strict scrutiny.[1] He explained how the current system works. First, a panel of officers is formed to review the personnel records of the men and women up for consideration. Let us assume, for the sake of illustration, that of a hundred people up for promotion, ten of them are black and ten are women. The panel's first job is to rank order the hundred from best to worst. If we assume that fifty people are to be promoted, then the top fifty people will be listed. But before the panel makes its final decision, it must ensure that women and minorities are represented in the final promotion list in at least the same proportion as they were represented on the list of all those eligible for promotion. In our example, since 10 percent of those up for promotion are black and another 10 percent are women, at least five blacks and five women must be promoted. If there are not at least five blacks and five women on the promotion list, then the promotion panel must drop white males on the bottom of the list to make room for the needed blacks and women. Of course, if there are enough or more than enough blacks or women on the promotion list, there is no need to go to the final step in the process. This is all done in the strictest secrecy. Because the original promotion lists are destroyed, it is never clear after the fact how many women or blacks would have been promoted without this special procedure. In

Captain Bigelow's opinion, these kinds of promotion systems could not stand up to strict scrutiny.

We can only assume that the other branches of the military and other agencies of the federal government operate under a similar system. These affirmative-preference plans are generally not going to withstand strict scrutiny: They are not temporary; they are not designed primarily to compensate for specific instances of past discrimination; and they are not narrowly tailored to achieve a specific result. Rather, they were created to bring about diversity at all levels of the federal bureaucracy.

In November 1995, the General Accounting Office (GAO) released a report which demonstrated that a higher percentage of women received promotions in the military when compared with blacks. The report, covering the years 1989 to 1993, was compiled at the request of Ron Dellums, a black Representative from Berkeley, California. The Clinton Defense Department promised to "correct" the problem and issue a new "Affirmative Action Planning and Assessment Process" program in the spring of 1996.

While the GAO report did not explain why a lower percentage of blacks were promoted when compared to women, the answer is obvious to anyone who has read Captain Bigelow's article. Apparently, in some situations, both women and blacks have been promoted without the need for the quota and this has happened more often for women than for blacks. Will the Clinton Defense Department's new affirmative action program, by ensuring that the quota is strictly adhered to in the future, guarantee that this imbalance never happens again? If so, will not the ultimate result be fewer promotions for women?

The vast majority of affirmative-preference programs in the United States were created in response to some kind of directive from Washington, D.C.; without it many would not have been created in the first place. Now that federal rules and regulations, and in most cases even federal statutes, may no longer be used to justify these plans, they will be viewed by federal judges as illegal race discrimination.

Once we remove all of the federal racial-preference programs, state and local governments will be left to ask themselves to what extent their own racial-preference programs stand up to the new standards imposed by the Court. State and local governments have not worried about that question in the past. Even though the Supreme Court ruled in 1989 that state and local affirmative-preference programs must withstand strict scrutiny, many of them were based in one way or another on requirements laid down by the federal government. For that reason, a large number of these programs have not been reviewed using the strict-scrutiny test. After the decision in *Adarand,* it is no longer possible for state and local governments to hide behind the federal government.

STATE AND LOCAL GOVERNMENT

First, what about programs that set aside a certain percentage of government contracts for business firms that are owned by the "right" minorities? In the *Croson* case the Supreme Court applied strict scrutiny to the minority set-aside program of Richmond, Virginia. This program had been established with little in the way of investigation to determine who actually had suffered from racial discrimination in the city's contracting program. Instead of spending the time and money it would have taken to actually figure out who had been the victims of race discrimination, Richmond's city council tried to take the easy way out by passing an ordinance requiring that 30 percent of all city contracts be given to firms owned by "Negroes, Spanish-speaking, Orientals, Indians, Eskimos, and Aleuts." The Supreme Court ruled against the plan. While it should have been clear after the *Croson* decision that such an effort to make up for some vague concept of discrimination would simply not pass strict scrutiny, many cities continued to maintain similar plans. In the years following this decision, federal appeals courts have struck down most city and state contract set-aside programs that have come up for review.

For example, in the 1991 case of *Coral Construction v. King County,* the Ninth Circuit Court ruled that King County, Washington's set-aside program did not live up to strict scrutiny.[2] For one thing, the plan attempted to help firms that had never done business in the county. The court ruled that since these kinds of plans are supposed to be remedial, they must focus on firms that might actually have suffered from past discrimination in the city or county in question. At the same time, because the county had extensive evidence of discrimination against some firms, it could have an affirmative-action program to aid firms which probably had actually suffered from past discrimination. In another 1991 case, *Milwaukee County Pavers v. Fiedler,* the Seventh Circuit Court ruled against Wisconsin's set-aside program.[3] The judges said that to simply "presume" that all blacks are "disadvantaged" is a "form of racial discrimination." They went on to say that "the whole point of *Croson* is that disadvantage, diversity, or other grounds for favoring minorities will not justify governmental racial discrimination...only a purpose of remedying discrimination against minorities will do that." After *Adarand,* we have to assume that federal, state, and local government regulations that presume minorities are disadvantaged will simply not withstand strict scrutiny.

In the 1992 case of *O'Donnell Construction v. District of Columbia,* the circuit court struck down the District of Columbia's set-aside program.[4] The plan reserved 35 percent of city contracts for minorities, and the court, finding no evidence of past discrimination against minorities, ruled that some kind of vague desire to remedy "societal discrimination" was not good enough to justify a racial-preference program. Also, the court could not understand why "Hispanics, Asians, Pacific Islanders and Native-Americans" were on the list of people to receive this special benefit, given the fact that the vast majority of minority businesses in the District of Columbia are owned by African Americans. The court said, "The random inclusion of racial groups for which there is no evidence of past discrimination in the construction industry raises doubts about the remedial nature of the set-aside program. In other words, if Richmond cannot have a vague plan that attempts to help the "usual list" of preferred minorities, neither can the District of Columbia or other cities and states.

In the 1993 case of *Contractors Association v. Philadelphia,* the Third Circuit Court of Appeals reviewed a similar set-aside program but did not declare the entire plan to be unconstitutional.[5] The court threw out that part of the program designed to help "Hispanics, Asians, and Native-Americans" because there were so few firms owned by these groups that it did not make sense to conclude that their lack of participation in the city contracting programs was the result of race discrimination. Actually, there were *no* firms owned by Native Americans in Philadelphia. The court did find that the city had enough evidence of past discrimination against black-owned firms to justify an affirmative-action plan to help them.

These cases demonstrate that the creation of contract set-aside plans that grant a racial preference to the "usual" list of preferred minorities are generally not going to withstand court review. However, plans that are created after significant research to correct a proven problem that had existed in the past for particular minority-owned firms in a particular city or county may withstand strict scrutiny.

In several cases in the early 1990s, state and local governments were able to defend their contract set-aside programs by arguing that they were simply implementing a federal mandate. In the 1991 case of *Tennessee Asphalt v. Ferris,* the Sixth Circuit Court upheld Tennessee's set-aside program because it was implementing the federal program.[6] The Second Circuit Court came to the same conclusion when reviewing New York's set-aside program in the 1992 case of *Harrison & Burrowes v. Cuomo.*[7] However, in that case the court also ruled that only the part of the program that was mandated by the federal government was legal; the part the state had created on its own was not. Now that federal set-aside programs must meet the same strict-scrutiny test, this is no longer a valid defense. Since these federal programs presume that certain groups are disadvantaged, they are now just as unconstitutional as similar state and local set-aside programs have been ruled to be.

What about racial-preference programs that attempt to ensure that enough minorities are hired or promoted by state and local government? In the 1990 case of *Long v. City of Saginaw,* the Sixth Circuit Court ruled that the city's affirmative-action plan did not live up to strict scrutiny.[8] Saginaw, Michigan, was trying to hire more minority police officers through an affirmative-action plan. Because there was no direct evidence of prior discrimination by the city, it tried to rely on statistics to prove that it had engaged in past discrimination. The court said: "It is only when the statistics disclose that the availability of minorities in the relevant labor pool substantially exceeded those hired that an inference of deliberate discrimination in employment may be drawn." The statistics in this case did not show a large enough difference between minorities in the labor pool and minorities on the police force to justify a race-based preference program.

In the 1992 case of *United Black Firefighter's Association v. Akron,* the Sixth Circuit Court threw out Akron, Ohio's plan to promote more blacks in the fire department to lieutenant.[9] While 76 percent of black firefighters and 89 percent of white ones passed the examination, only six blacks were in the top fifty. Since the city planned to promote only fifty people to lieutenant, only six blacks would make it if the city went down the list in rank order. The city proposed to go down the list to number fifty-nine to pick up four more blacks. The court ruled that this was simply "racial preference" and could not stand up to strict scrutiny. There was no evidence of past intentional discrimination on the part of the city, and the desire to overcome societal discrimination did not suffice to meet the test.

In 1993, the Sixth Circuit Court reviewed Detroit's affirmative-action plan to hire and promote more black police officers in the case of *Detroit Police Officer's Association v. Young.*[10] The city had adopted a plan nineteen years before in an effort to achieve a fifty-fifty ratio of black to white officers and sergeants. By 1993 more than 50 percent of the city's patrolmen and sergeants were black. The court ordered Detroit to end its affirmative-action plan, since it had met its stated goals. While this plan once served a "compelling" purpose, that purpose had been achieved.

The Fourth Circuit Court came to a similar conclusion in the 1993 case of *Maryland Troopers Association v. Evans.*[11] The Maryland attorney general had found that the Maryland state police examination process had been rigged so that those at the top could help their personal friends win promotions. Because these top officers and their friends were white, the rigging helped white troopers achieve promotion, not blacks. The state stopped the rigging and set up a promotion quota for black troopers. The Fourth Circuit Court threw out the quota system, finding that this manipulation of examination results was not an example of past intentional discrimination by government. Also, there was no "gross statistical disparity" between minority troopers and troopers promoted. From 1980 to 1991, the percentage of black troopers had gone from 9.5 to 17.1 percent, and by 1991, 10 percent of the sergeants were black. The court said that this statistical disparity, absent more proof, was not enough to prove discrimination. Judge Wilkinson, writing for the court, said:

> The case against race-based preference does not rest upon the sterile assumption that American society is untouched or unaffected by the tragic oppression of its past. Rather, it is the very enormity of that tragedy that lends resolve to the desire never to repeat it, and to find a legal order in which distinctions based on race shall have no place.

While many states and cities had gross statistical disparities in traditionally segregated job categories in the 1960s and 1970s, that was no longer true for most of them in the 1990s. It is therefore reasonable to assume that most of the state and local affirmative-action hiring and promotion plans that still give preferences based on race could not stand up to strict scrutiny.

This is particularly true in the case of public schools and state universities that have been openly trying to create faculties where the ratio of minority teachers comes closer to the ratio of minority students on campus. While Justice Stevens felt that this kind of "role model" affirmative-action program was acceptable, a majority of the justices of the Supreme Court have never agreed with him. In the past, many public schools and state universities, at the insistence of the federal government, tried to hire faculty using the "role-model" theory, but it is now clear that the federal government's efforts to achieve this goal would not stand up to strict scrutiny. In other words, as a result of *Adarand,* these kinds of affirmative-action plans are not constitutional.

Take the 1990 case of *Cunico v. Pueblo School District No. 60*.[12] Connie Cunico, a white social worker, sued because the school district laid her off but did not lay off a less senior black social worker. The school district argued that it was trying to keep its only black social worker in order to have more diversity on the workforce. The Tenth Circuit Court applied strict scrutiny, and this so-called affirmative-action plan did not withstand the test. There was no evidence that the school district had discriminated in the past against black employees. Any goal other than to compensate for past discrimination is not compelling and does not meet strict scrutiny. The school district had to rehire Connie Cunico.

Throughout the 1980s and into the 1990s state universities have tried to increase the number of minority faculty members, often with little success because of the lack of minorities holding Ph.D.'s in the desired field. Such efforts are generally not going to live up to the strict-scrutiny test, either.

Two affirmative-preference plans upheld in 1994 illustrate the kinds of plans that are going to withstand strict scrutiny. In *Peightal v. Dade County,* the Eleventh Circuit Court found that Dade County, Florida, had very convincing statistical evidence to prove that blacks and Hispanics had been the victims of race discrimination in the past when it came to hiring for the fire department.[13] The county had tried other methods to bring more blacks and Hispanics into the department but they had failed. Finally, the county created a program that gave a preference to blacks and Hispanics even if they did not score as high on the entrance exam as other applicants. With strong evidence that the exam was racially biased against minorities, the court ruled that Dade County could continue to employ an affirmative-preference program to compensate for that racial bias and to make up for proven, past racial discrimination.

In *Edwards v. City of Houston,* the Fifth Circuit Court was faced with a similar case of proven past discrimination against blacks and Hispanics by the Houston police department.[14] Since the examinations used to promote police officers to sergeant and lieutenant were clearly biased, the court allowed the city to establish quotas that would ensure that a particular percentage of black and Hispanic police officers were promoted.

These two racial-preference plans withstood strict scrutiny because Houston and Dade County could point to specific examples of past discrimination or statistics which were so egregious that it was reasonable to conclude that intentional race discrimination had occurred in the past. They could also argue that quotas were needed to compensate for examinations that were racially biased.

GOVERNMENTS AND SEX DISCRIMINATION

How the Supreme Court is ultimately going to deal with affirmative action for women is a different question. In the 1970s the Supreme Court developed a different test to judge whether or not sex discrimination violated the concept of equal protection in order to accommodate affirmative-preference programs that benefited women. This test only requires that the reason be "important," not "compelling." Also, the affirmative-action plan for women does not have to be "narrowly tailored." It is not clear exactly what is required in the way of tailoring when it comes to affirmative-preference programs for women.

This "different" test for sex discrimination as opposed to race discrimination has more to do with the evolution of legal thinking than with any logical justification. During the twentieth century the Supreme Court came to see "race" discrimination as the most potentially destructive act a government could perform. Because of that, any attempt to discriminate on the basis of race had to withstand "strict scrutiny" and most governmental actions could not pass that test. The same liberal justices who were so concerned with race discrimination were less sensitive to the problem of sex discrimination. It was easier for them to imagine that physical differences could account for different treatment of the sexes at the hands of government at all levels. Because of this, they developed a lower standard for sex discrimination. Moreover, when the Supreme Court first encountered race discrimination, there was no such thing as affirmative-action programs for minorities. By the time the Court began to develop the standard of review for sex discrimination, it was faced early on with efforts by governments to make up for past discrimination against women. The lower standard of review was designed with this in mind.

The federal circuit courts have acknowledged that the test for gender-based affirmative action is different than for race-based affirmative action. In the 1987 case of *Associated General Contractors v. City of San Francisco,* the Ninth Circuit Court threw out San Francisco's contract set-aside program for minorities.[15] Because there was no evidence of past racial discrimination by the city, the minority set-aside program did not survive strict scrutiny. At the same time the Court, turning to the gender-based affirmative action set-aside program, said that affirmative action for women raised "some of the most difficult and sensitive questions" and that the so-called mid-level review that the Supreme Court had developed for these plans provided "relatively little guidance in individual cases." The Ninth Circuit Court then upheld the city's program to help women-owned firms obtain city contracts. The court found that the plan was "substantially related to the city's important goal of compensating women for the disparate treatment they have suffered in the marketplace."

On the other hand, other circuit courts have not found that similar programs in other cities and states meet even this lower test. In the 1993 case of *Contractors Association v. Philadelphia,* the Third Circuit Court, while it found that Philadelphia's set-aside plan for blacks met strict scrutiny, did not believe that the city's plan to help women with a similar program could even stand up to the lower standard of scrutiny such plans must meet.

This question of whether or not cities, states, and the federal government are going to be allowed to have affirmative action for women but not for minorities raises many difficult issues. For many people, the thought that the daughter of a millionaire from the Upper East Side of Manhattan can benefit from affirmative action, while the son of a black blue-collar worker from Harlem cannot, is going to be difficult to take. On the other hand, is the Supreme Court ready to move women into the higher category and say that sex discrimination must meet the same strict scrutiny that race discrimination must meet? Justice O'Connor has been trying to move the Supreme Court in that direction since she joined the Court in 1981. It remains to be seen whether or not she can convince four of her colleagues that the time has come to give women full equality under the concept of equal protection. The Court may well make this change in a case involving affirmative action for women but not minorities that seems particularly unfair to minorities.

STATE UNIVERSITIES AND THEIR STUDENTS

While the decisions in *Croson* and *Adarand* will bring an end to many of the affirmative-action programs of cities, states, and the federal government, they will not affect the student-admissions policies of state universities, at least not directly. Until the Supreme Court speaks again to this issue, these decisions will still be ruled by *Bakke*. It is important to remember, however, that this was not a decision in which five justices agreed. Four justices wanted Bakke admitted, and four did not. Four justices approved of affirmative action based on race in admissions, and four refused to discuss the constitutional issue. The decision that has ruled admissions decisions by state universities since 1978 was signed by only one justice. Nevertheless, until overturned, that decision stands as the law of the land. Justice Powell said that state universities may not have a two-track admission system but may take factors such as race into account in order to achieve a more diverse student body. This was the only affirmative-action decision based on a desire by the Court to achieve diversity that has not been overturned.

While *Bakke* is still law, the Supreme Court refused to review a decision by the Fourth Circuit Court at the same time it handed down the *Adarand* decision. This left the circuit court's decision intact. In the 1994 case of *Podberesky v. Kirwan*, a Hispanic student sued when he found that he was not allowed to compete for scholarships at the University of Maryland that were reserved for black students.[16] The university argued that it needed the race-based scholarship program for four reasons: first, to help overcome the university's poor reputation in the African-American community; second, to help remedy an underrepresentation of African-American students in the student body; third, to help correct the low retention and graduation rates of African-American students; and fourth, to help remedy an atmosphere that is perceived to be hostile to African-American students.

Because the federal district judge found all these conditions to exist, he upheld the race-based scholarship program. The Fourth Circuit Court overturned this decision after subjecting the program to strict scrutiny. This was not a narrowly tailored program designed to overcome the effects of past discrimination by the university. The court ruled that the university failed to prove that the current problems were the result of past discrimination or were of sufficient magnitude to justify this particular program; it also rejected the idea that the first and last reasons could ever justify this kind of race-based program. While the need to attract and retain more African-American students might have justified the program, there was no evidence that African-American students would come or stay longer because of it. The court was unhappy that the scholarship program was open to students from any part of the country rather than being targeted to students that might have actually suffered from past discrimination at the hands of the university. The university argued that it needed to attract top African-American students to act as role models for other such students. The circuit court pointed out that the need to create role models had never been an acceptable reason for race-based actions by the government. The Supreme Court's refusal to review the decision suggests that similar race-based scholarship programs at state universities around the country will also fail to meet the strict-scrutiny test.

The Supreme Court may well overturn *Bakke,* or at least modify its ruling, because of a case currently working its way through the federal appeals process, *Hopwood v. the University of Texas School of Law.*[17] Cheryl Hopwood, a white woman, brought the case after her application was rejected and she discovered that minorities with lower grade-point averages and test scores had been admitted. Upon closer examination, she found that the law school was operating a two-track admissions system in clear violation of Justice Powell's decision in *Bakke*. She also found that the law school's affirmative-action program was restricted to African Americans and Mexican Americans.

The law school first explained that it was trying to make up for past racial discrimination. Cheryl Hopwood and her attorneys did not buy that for several reasons. First of all, the law school had been found guilty in the 1940s of discriminating against African Americans living in Texas. Most of the African Americans admitted under this affirmative-action plan were from outside the state of Texas. Second, there was no evidence of past intentional discrimination against Mexican Americans. The federal district judge ruled that the law school could continue to operate an affirmative-action program as long as it stopped the two-track system and as long as the goal was diversity, which was the law school's second explanation for its plan. The problem with that explanation is that the law school's plan did not attempt to help Hispanics in general or other minority groups, such as Native Americans or Vietnamese Americans. It only helped African Americans and Mexican Americans—which Justice Powell did not discuss in his opinion. Who decides how much diversity is enough, and is it acceptable to have a diversity-based plan that only helps a few minority groups?

Critics of the University of Texas School of Law argued that what was clearly happening was racial politics. The law school had a special admissions program for African Americans and Mexican Americans because of their political power in the state legislature, the body that decides how much state funding the law school receives. If that is the real explanation of what was going on in the law school, it is clearly not a legitimate reason to discriminate on the basis of race.

On August 8, 1995, the case was argued before the Fifth Circuit Court of Appeals in New Orleans. During two hours of argument the judges asked the law school's attorney a number of pointed questions. They wanted to know how many African American and Hispanic students would have been admitted without the affirmative-preference plan. The answer was nine

African Americans and eighteen Hispanics for the entering class in 1992. One judge commented that this amounted to "some" diversity. Another judge pointed out that no Native Americans were admitted by the law school in 1992 in an entering class of five hundred. He wondered out loud how that could be called successful diversification. Overhanging *Hopwood* was the famous case of *Sweatt v. Painter* in which the Supreme Court, in 1950, ordered the University of Texas School of Law to admit blacks for the first time.[18] When the law school's attorney argued that the rejected white students could always attend some other law school, one of the judges commented: "That's exactly what the state of Texas told Mr. Sweatt."

As of this writing the Fifth Circuit Court had not handed down a decision in *Hopwood*. Regardless of what the circuit court decides, the U.S. Supreme Court may well take the opportunity provided by this case to return to *Bakke* and the issue of intentional "affirmative" race discrimination by state universities. Since no five justices could agree on a single opinion, the Court will be free to examine the issue without being bound in any way by the *Bakke* decision.

THE FUTURE OF GOVERNMENT AFFIRMATIVE ACTION

Lost in much of the rhetoric surrounding the issue of affirmative action is the fact that hiring and promotion quotas and race-and-sex conscious remedies were supposed to be temporary. At some point they were supposed to go away. Nothing illustrates this better than the 1994 case of *Ensley Branch, NAACP v. Seibels*.[19] Birmingham, Alabama, has been under some kind of court order to integrate its workforce, both by race and sex, since 1974. Finally, in the 1990s, the minorities and women who have been subject to various affirmative-action plans for two decades asked the federal courts to move them to the next stage. What is the next stage? They asked that the judges order Birmingham to come up with valid criteria for hiring and promotion that did not discriminate against minorities or women. The Eleventh Circuit Court ordered Birmingham to do just that. Judge Carnes pointed out what should be obvious to everyone: that giving tests which blacks and women fail and then promoting them outside the usual process is the next best thing to actual discrimination for someone who wants to discriminate. It stigmatizes the people involved without getting to the real issue of whether or not they can really do the work. Judge Carnes said:

> Under its present decree, the Board may indefinitely administer racially discriminatory tests and then attempt to cure the resulting injury to blacks with race-conscious affirmative action. Federal courts should not tolerate such institutionalized discrimination.... Use of racial hiring quotas to mask the effects of discriminatory selection procedures places grievous burdens on blacks as well as whites.

Judge Carnes pointed out that other cities had been able to come up with valid tests for selecting people to be police and firefighters that did not discriminate against women or minorities; he did not see why Birmingham could not do the same. He said: "We cannot allow stopgap remedies to turn into permanent palliatives."

This decision points out the major flaw with too many government affirmative-action plans based on race or sex. They refuse to deal with the long-term problem, which is a selection and promotion process that is biased and tests that are not valid. The next step in the affirmative-action process is to make sure that the selection and promotion process is fair; that tests and other criteria are unbiased and actually predict future performance on the job. It is time for most cities, states, and the federal government to move on to that next step.

AFFIRMATIVE ACTION BY PRIVATE EMPLOYERS

Most private employers have paid very little attention to the legal requirements of the Supreme Court when it comes to their own affirmative-action plans because they were created at the demand of the OFCC; the employers have assumed they could use that fact as a defense in a reverse-discrimination case. With the Supreme Court's decision that the federal government must meet the same strict-scrutiny test that state and local governments must meet, the rules promulgated by the OFCC are probably no longer valid. Private employers who have their own affirmative action plans are on their own.

The Supreme Court laid down the rules that apply to private employers in 1979 with the *Weber* decision and in 1987 with the *Johnson* decision.[20] Race- and gender-conscious affirmative-preference plans are allowed when they are needed to "break down old patterns of" segregation or when there is a "significant underrepresentation" of women or minorities in a "traditionally segregated job classification." The reality is that the vast majority of private employers can no longer meet that test. Most have been successful in breaking down old patterns of segregation and no longer have a significant underrepresentation of women or minorities in a traditionally segregated job classification. This should be cause for celebration, but it may not be in many circles because it means private employers must also go to the next level and must concern themselves with making sure their hiring and promotion procedures are fair. They were supposed to do so in the 1960s, but the existence of OFCC regulations and affirmative action allowed this all-important goal to be postponed. It cannot be postponed any longer.

THE LAW AS IT STANDS

American society has become comfortable with the crutch of affirmative action. But the reality is that affirmative-preference programs based on race and gender were never meant to be a permanent way of life. They were intended to be a temporary measure to move American society forward. We could argue about whether or not now is the time to end affirmative-preference programs, but it would be a waste of time. It is time to move past goals and quotas toward real fairness in contracting, hiring, and promotions. The Supreme Court has ruled. America must get on with the job.

9

FROM PREFERENCE
TO FAIRNESS

Booker T. Washington, W. E. B. Du Bois, Malcolm X, and Martin Luther King Jr. did not invent or even endorse the idea of affirmative preference. While African-American leaders such as these had different ideas about how to advance the cause of freedom and equality for African Americans, none of them thought that establishing some kind of special preference based on race was the answer. What is wrong with racial preference?

We know that in the first few years of affirmative preference at the University of California at Davis Medical School, only a third of those who benefited from affirmative preference were black. While we have no statistics on the subject, it is generally believed that during the 1980s and into the 1990s the vast majority of affirmative-preference hirings and promotions went to white women, Hispanics, and Asians, not to African Americans. Yet when Americans attach a stigma to a group based on their need for affirmative-preference programs, they do not talk about white women, Hispanics, or Asians but about African Americans. It is African Americans who complain that everyone assumes they got where they are because of affirmative preference. Only a black man, Steven L. Carter, could write a book calling himself an "affirmative-action baby."[1] It is successful blacks who are assumed to be products of affirmative preference, not successful Asians. As black leaders such as Ward Connerly and Shelby Steele have pointed out, to the extent affirmative-preference programs stigmatize black Americans, it is not a very good deal for them. They get little concrete benefit in exchange for being stigmatized.

What people call affirmative preference has too often been in reality some form of corrupt decision making in which someone's personal friend got the job, the promotion, or the tenure. If that personal friend happened to be other than a white man, then affirmative preference could be the excuse for making the decision outside the "normal" process. No one felt comfortable criticizing this "extraordinary" procedure; to do so would be considered an attack on civil rights. Anyone criticizing the process would be labeled a racist or a sexist. Often the person who would have gotten the job or promotion if a fair decision process had been used was a more qualified woman or minority. The net result was that an incompetent woman or minority found success through corruption, while a competent woman or minority achieved failure. Because the corrupt choice was incompetent, all women and minorities suffered from the stigma created by affirmative preference.

The unmistakable reality is that affirmative preference is racist and sexist and breeds racism and sexism. In 1995 those whose ancestors settled Hawaii before whites (or Asians) arrived there asked to be classed as Native Americans rather than Asians, believing that affirmative action for Asians would soon come to an end. Which is reminiscent of the man in *Plessy v. Ferguson* who kept protesting that he was seven-eighths white and deserved to sit in the White's Only railroad car.[2]

Because many Hispanics in America have intermarried with other races, some people now argue that a new category called "mixed-race Hispanic" should be created to deal with such individuals. We have to wonder how mixed someone will have to be to qualify as a mixed-race Hispanic. What about other people who are of mixed ancestry? Where will they fit into the "government by racial preference" scheme?

The unspoken reality is that affirmative preference violates the fundamental principles of America. American society was built on ideas such as democracy, individual freedom, political equality, and economic opportunity. The affirmative-preference programs of the last three decades of the twentieth century have violated all of these principles. Throughout these decades, in poll after poll, a majority of all voting-age Americans have expressed their dissatisfaction with affirmative-preference programs. Apparently, if a vote had been taken, the people would have voted against such programs. Yet America's leaders decided they knew what was best for the "ignorant" citizens of the world's greatest democracy. There is a particularly appalling kind of arrogance about that idea. The Supreme Court justices who wrote the decisions in *Dred Scott v. Sandford* in 1857 and *Plessy v. Ferguson* in 1896 also knew what was "best" for America.[3] Civil War and racial segregation were the result.

Ultimately, there cannot be democracy without some guidance from the people. Congress has refused to pass a general statute dealing with affirmative action. Without the legislative debate and open fact-finding that accompany a statutory change, the American people have been prevented from knowing the full reach of this policy. In a democracy this cannot go on forever.

Throughout the debate over affirmative preference one side has talked about the need to protect "equal opportunity," while the other side has talked about the "myth" of equal opportunity. In a very real sense both sides have been right. When the public universities of a state such as California decide that they will do whatever it takes to graduate more minorities, even to the point of reducing the level of instruction, no one is served. While a few more minorities may begin life with a piece of paper that says they are educated, the world will soon discover that the paper is worthless. Justice Brennan's argument in favor of educational affirmative preference was that some students should be given a chance to fairly compete. If they can perform well in school and pass tests given at the end of each class, then any entrance exam that indicated they could not do so would clearly be specious. But if the classroom tests are not valid, then we can never know if the entrance exam was a worthy indicator or not. We can never know if affirmative preference is a way of compensating for what is in reality an unfair admissions process or just racism in reverse.

While the idea that "two wrongs don't make a right" is simplistic, it also has a ring of truth. Certainly some people are given unfair preferences in life. The children of wealthy alumni will always have a place reserved for them at America's top universities. As long as those universities depend on alumni contributions for their financial survival, it is not realistic to expect that this will ever change. At the same time, there are other preferences that can be changed. The major obstacle to the promotion of women in government agencies is preferences for veterans, which made sense through much of the twentieth century. Early in the century it was argued that men who had military experience would understand better how government "works" and therefore make better civil servants. Now that government is trying to move away from the hierarchical structure of the past, that argument no longer makes much sense. Later in the century, it was maintained that men who had volunteered to risk their lives for their country with little compensation should be given a helping hand. At the end of the century, with what is supposed to be a professional military, this contention is less convincing. Professional soldiers are supposed to be compensated fairly with pay and benefits while they serve, not after the fact. Instead of trying to pile one preference on top of another, women would be better served if they would work for an end to all preferences not based on competence. Society would also be better served to the extent that the best person actually occupied every government job.

When President Carter thought that the Supreme Court was about to put an end to affirmative preference, his administration drafted a plan to modify preferences for veterans in order to make the government employment process fairer for women. His plan called for a veteran to enjoy preference for a specific period of years after leaving the military to help him or her in adjusting to civilian life. That plan was scrapped when the Supreme Court upheld the affirmative-action plans at issue. The Supreme Court has finally done in 1995 what President Carter thought it might do in the late 1970s, and it is time to examine the whole issue of preferences granted by federal and state governments.

In an attempt to deal with the fact that less than half of their African-American and Hispanic students actually graduate, many large state universities have lowered admission standards to increase the number of such students on campus. The rather mindless attitude seems to be that if half make it through and we would like a particular number to graduate each year, then by increasing the number who begin the process we will get the desired result.

Because of the untouchable nature of the subject of affirmative action, very few studies have been done on the minority dropout rate at most major universities. One study at the University of Maryland found that minorities drop out in two waves.[4] The first wave leaves in the first year because they cannot do the work academically. Presumably, many of the "lower admission standard" students simply swell this first wave of dropouts. However, many minority students do not flunk out in the first year. They are capable of doing college-level work. Interviews found that they leave because college is not much "fun" for them. Because of their financial reality, they cannot afford to live on or near campus. They also have to work many hours a week away from campus. As a result, they do not make friends at school and do not participate in any campus activities. In other words, they do not have much of a "college experience." If we really wanted to help these students graduate, we would provide financial assistance that would make it possible for them to live on campus without the need to work long hours for low pay in order to make ends meet. They would make friends and attend campus functions, and college would be more fun for them. Scholarships and loans would cover tuition and other costs, or they could work one semester and go to college the next.

The point is that affirmative preference has been an expedient procedural device enabling governments to "pretend" to deal with what is still a very serious problem. Such programs have done some harm and some good. The Supreme Court has ruled that they must come to an end. Whether or not we agree with the Supreme Court that now is the time to end them, that is the reality. Busing to achieve racial integration in public schools achieved a little integration over the short term. There is not much else it can accomplish given today's reality of where people live, and it is being replaced with magnet schools and other special programs that seem to be succeeding. The same is true of affirmative-preference programs. They helped integrate some organizations faster than any other method available, but now other methods must be used. We must move from preference to fairness.

To demonstrate the limits of affirmative-preference programs, we have only to look at the number of minorities at the nation's top "liberal" magazines. In the March 13, 1995, issue of the *Nation,* Katha Pollitt pointed out:

> In the 13 years I've been associated with the *Nation,* we have had exactly one nonwhite person (briefly) on our editorial staff of 13, despite considerable turnover. And we're not alone: the *Atlantic* has zero nonwhites out of an editorial staff of 21; *Harper's,* zero out of 14; the *New York Review of Books,* zero out of nine; the *Utne Reader,* zero out of 12. A few do a little better, although nothing to cheer about: the *Progressive,* one out of six; *Mother Jones,* one out of seven; *In These Times,* one out of nine; the *New Republic,* two out of 22; the *New Yorker,* either three or six, depending on how you define "editorial," out of 100 plus...[5]

After a quarter century of affirmative preference the liberal media, which has so delighted in pointing the finger of blame at everyone else, is a classic example of how far some people have come and how far some people have yet to go. If this is the best these bastions of affirmative preference can do after three decades, perhaps it is time to try something else.

CONGRESS

During the 1970s and 1980s, Congress passed a lot of small affirmative-preference provisions while refusing to deal with the issue in a general way with hearings and a major "affirmative action" statute. A few of the provisions directly mandated affirmative preference, such as the law creating the set-aside programs for government contracts. Most tried to encourage affirmative preference in a variety of ways. For example, when the FCC expressed a desire to reexamine its own affirmative-preference programs, Congress placed a provision in the appropriations bill that forbade the agency from using any money for such a reexamination.[6] None of these affirmative-preference programs would stand up to strict scrutiny, which requires Congress to conduct true fact-finding, analyze the specific discrimination it wishes to eliminate, and then develop a "temporary" plan to deal with that specific problem. Congress has never done this in the past and is probably not capable of doing it in the future. So what should Congress do now? It should repeal all the affirmative-preference provisions and get them off the books. The Supreme Court has made them all null and void with its decision in *Adarand Constructors v. Pena,* and Congress could help us all to face that fact by taking them off the books.

POLITICS

Many politicians have made a career out of the politics of race and it is time for racial politics to come to an end. At the end of the 1995 Texas legislative session, Gov. George Bush Jr. said that Texans had rejected the politics of race. He was referring to the fact that the Texas legislature had rejected a number of proposals to expand affirmative-preference programs in Texas. Most of these proposed programs would not have withstood strict scrutiny and would have been illegal when passed. But it is wonderful to hear a governor of a former member of the Confederate States of America say that the people of that state have finally rejected the politics of race. His father was elected to the presidency in 1988 by using race. Wouldn't it be wonderful if we could get past racial politics? That is certainly what many leaders of the past, from Martin Luther King Jr. to Lyndon Johnson, had hoped for. Now is the time to make it a reality.

THE FEDERAL BUREAUCRACY

Major changes must come from the federal bureaucracy. During President Reagan's eight years there were many debates concerning whether or not he should amend the affirmative-action executive orders signed by Presidents Kennedy and Johnson.[7] There is no need to amend them, since none require anyone to institute an affirmative-preference program. On their face they call for affirmative recruitment and affirmative fairness, not affirmative preference. The bureaucrats created the world of goals and timetables that American business came to know and love. Those regulations could all be rescinded without any violation of either statutes or executive orders.

What if all the thousands of federal bureaucrats who have tried to teach Americans how to institute affirmative-preference programs now turned their attention to actually helping people institute affirmative-fairness programs? Given decades of experience, many cities have learned how to conduct fair hiring and promotion exams for police and fire departments. Couldn't federal bureaucrats gather and distribute that information? Surely we know much about which kinds of tests are biased and in what way. Thus far, as of this writing, there is no sign that the federal bureaucracy has the intention of doing any such thing.

In the early 1980s the EEOC began to give awards to companies that demonstrated they could achieve affirmative fairness. The list of the companies that have received the awards is very long and includes many of the largest companies in America, from Anheuser-Busch to Polaroid, from Marriott to Westing-house, and from Procter & Gamble to Johnson & Johnson. These companies have instituted special programs, such as mentoring, to help women and minorities move up the corporate ladder. They have also increased their outreach into minority communities. In other words, the federal bureaucracy knows a lot about affirmative recruitment and affirmative fairness. It is time for it to share that knowledge with the rest of us.

Take the way the military currently uses quotas to promote people up through the ranks. It assumes that racism and sexism exist in the military structure of the United States and uses quotas to compensate for that assumed bias. Is that still a reasonable assumption in the second half of the 1990s? Isn't it time to find out just how much racism and sexism is left in the military? The current promotion procedure requires a panel to rank people from best to worst and then promote the required number by moving down from the top. Then adjustments are made if there are not "enough" women and minorities on the promotion list. Since all this is done in secret, we do not know how many adjustments have been made over the years. Now it is time to find out. A new procedure might require anyone who is up for promotion and who believes he or she is a victim of racism or sexism to report that to the appropriate office. That charge would be investigated, and both the charge and the result of the investigation could become part of the promotion file. Instead of assuming the effects of racism and sexism, the promotion panel could then know exactly how racism and sexism had affected a particular person's career. Of course, that promotion panel must include some women and minorities. In one sense, the major benefit of having gone through a period of affirmative preference is that we now have women and minorities who have moved up through the ranks of the military so that the panels can now include people from a wide variety of backgrounds to help make these difficult decisions.

Fairness is more difficult than preference. It may mean that in some cases fewer minorities or women get promotions, but the opposite is also true. Freed from the strict quota, it may mean that more minorities and women receive promotions. It is highly probable that as long as the preference system was in place, there would seldom have been more than the required number of minorities and women promoted by each panel.

During the summer of 1995, the Justice Department released a thirty-seven-page memorandum asking all federal agencies to conduct a study of their affirmative-action programs to see if they could survive strict scrutiny after the *Adarand* decision.[8] What is there to study? None of the federal government's current affirmative-preference programs, whether created by statute, administrative fiat, or executive order, could withstand strict scrutiny.

THE PRESIDENT

There is no substitute for presidential leadership in this difficult area. America cannot afford to spend the next decade bogged down in thousands of reverse-discrimination lawsuits as preference gives way to fairness slowly and with much pain. It would be better for all concerned if the entire nation made the transition as quickly as possible. This will take leadership. It is not a question of partisan politics. Many of the most prominent Republicans were as involved in creating the current system of preference as the Democrats. The Civil Rights Acts of 1972 and 1991 were passed with a large measure of support from both parties. These two laws made the preference system possible. What's more, it is common knowledge that Congress buried dozens of little preference provisions in things like appropriations bills. No one who served in Congress during those years can claim ignorance of what happened to affirmative action at the federal level.

Whomever the American citizenry elects as president in 1996, that person must move the society forward on this issue. It would be reasonable to ask the presidential candidates how, beyond vague rhetoric and general pronouncements, they intend to do that. How will they help us require affirmative-fairness programs of federal contractors? How will the programs be judged? How many resources will they devote to this important task? What is their concept of fairness in the workplace? All are relevant questions in 1996.

STATE AND LOCAL GOVERNMENTS

We also need leadership from governors, mayors, legislators, and other elected officials. The affirmative-preference programs at the state and local level must be transformed as much as those at the federal level. Quotas, goals, timetables, and set-asides must give way to programs designed to make sure that everyone, including women and minorities, has a fair chance at government jobs and government contracts. One of the rationales for contract set-aside programs has been that new, small businesses have higher expenses for such items as insurance and therefore cannot compete with larger firms. If that is true, then state and local governments could institute a set-aside program for new small businesses. A business that is less than ten years old and has fewer than a hundred employees could go on the small-business register and stay there for some period of years. During that time some contracts would be put up for bid only by the companies on the small-business register. That means that all the bidding companies would have the same problems with insurance costs that keep them from competing in the government contract market. A special program for small businesses could be viewed as a training program, and when the training period was over, these companies would understand how the process works and be able to move into the regular competition. More than half of all the new small businesses created in the first half of the 1990s were created by women and minorities. A program to help new small enterprises would help many businesses owned by women and minorities without the stigma attached to special programs that give preferences based on race or sex.

JOB TESTING

Everyone involved in the process of reviewing job tests must take a more realistic view of what they are capable of telling us about potential success or failure on the job. In the 1981 case of *Johnson v. Santa Clara County,* Paul Johnson had a score of 77, and Diane Joyce had a score of 75.[9] The scores were the result of an interview and evaluation by a panel of people. Even the most sophisticated tests have an error factor of plus or minus 2 or 3 points. In other words, there is no practical difference between a 77 and a 75. To conclude that Paul Johnson was somehow more qualified for the job on the basis of his test score was ludicrous.

Too often tests that might be useful in separating the highly qualified from the qualified and the unqualified are used instead to come up with a rank order of candidates. It would make much more sense to use them to create groups of job candidates. If there is one opening, then that person could be selected at random from the list of highly qualified candidates. There is nothing in law or science which says that people have to be selected based on their score on a test that cannot make fine distinctions between individuals. If there were many openings, then the jobs would go first to those who were in the highly qualified group. Others would be chosen at random from the qualified category once everyone in the highly qualified category had been chosen. Choices based on random selection from a group of qualified people would be fairer than the current system and more likely to select a significant number of women and minorities.

Many businesses and government agencies have argued that they cannot come up with "job-valid" tests. That is not true. It means giving people tests and then seeing how they actually perform on the job. If there is a strong positive correlation between the test score and job performance, then the test is valid. If there is not, the test is not valid.

We have a long history on this subject from the military. In one case the military had a new machine, and it wanted to find out who could operate it with the least number of errors. The military gave a group of soldiers an IQ test and then put them into the training program to learn how to operate this machine. The result was that people with low IQs made too many mistakes because they could not understand the complex machine; those with high IQs made too many mistakes because they got bored. Soldiers with mid-level IQs proved ideal. The only way to figure that out was to put a lot of different kinds of people on the machine and test their performance.

UNIVERSITIES

Could university admissions move from preference to fairness? Of course, and there are two basic approaches: A university might use entrance-exam scores and high school grades to admit the top students and reject the bottom ones. The in-between students could then either be evaluated in depth or selected at random. A random selection of students from those deemed to be "qualified for admission" would be fairer than the current system and still allow many minorities to be admitted to college. If evaluation in depth is the method of selection, then admissions committees would have to ask a lot of difficult questions. Which students have had to overcome more than their share of obstacles to graduate from high school? Which students have talents that compensate for their lower academic performance, at least at the admission stage? Which students have a particular weakness which, if overcome, might result in better performance? Can summer programs help to overcome those weaknesses? These questions can be answered, and if they were, a fairer admissions process would result.

The Rutgers University Law School in Newark, New Jersey, has had an affirmative-action program based on fairness rather than preference for many years. First of all, they admit the "regular class," using the standard criteria, such as grades and test scores. Then the admissions officers examine the records of other applicants to see if they deserve special consideration. They look for evidence that the student has had to overcome obstacles to get a college degree. If they believe that the applicant has the potential to perform in law school with a little extra help, the applicant is admitted through the special program. Some white students have been admitted through this program, although most have been minorities. There are special summer sessions for such students to help them learn how to study for law-school exams and how to work with other students in order to understand the material. The Rutgers University Law School has had great success with its program. Most of the students in the special-admissions program have graduated. In 1970 there were ten thousand lawyers in New Jersey, and less than a hundred were nonwhite. In 1990 there were two thousand black, Hispanic, and Asian lawyers in New Jersey; 40 percent of them had come from the Rutgers University Law School's special program.

Sara Manzano is one of the program's success stories. She was born the fourth of six children of Puerto Rican immigrants in a Harlem housing project. As someone who could speak English, she learned to represent her family and friends before government agencies. Bringing her into law school was natural, given her history as an advocate. Sara Manzano is now an attorney with the Department of Housing and Urban Development. It is hard to imagine anyone who would be more qualified to work in that arena. Rutgers University Law School did well to see in her the special qualities that are needed to be an effective attorney and to disregard some deficiencies that were caused by her life experiences.[10]

At the same time, even the Rutgers program has potential problems in light of recent Supreme Court decisions. The way the program is currently run, anyone who is a minority is presumed to be disadvantaged, while whites must *prove* that they are. Federal courts have said that this assumption cannot stand up to the strict-scrutiny test. That means Rutgers and other universities with similar programs around the country must change the way they define disadvantaged in the years to come. Middle-class minorities will no longer be eligible for special consideration. At the same time, minorities and whites who have really had to overcome major obstacles in life will still be eligible for a special-admissions program.

BEYOND PREFERENCE

Going beyond preference will not be easy. Too many people have gotten used to the easy way of dealing with a difficult issue. The federal courts stand ready and willing to do the job of forcing the society to move from preference to fairness. Personally, I lived through another period when the federal courts were asked to accomplish that kind of task alone. Public schools were integrated, but with a great deal of pain for everyone involved. The same thing can happen in this area without leadership from governors and presidents. Elected officials can stick their heads in the sand and let the storm break around them, or they can do what they get paid to do—lead.

10

WHAT'S WRONG WITH DIVERSITY?

The admissions officer at an Ivy League university says proudly that her school is committed to 100 percent diversity. What does that mean? Presumably, that some minority students who would not otherwise have had a chance to attend the university will be enrolled in each entering class. It also means that the school practices discrimination in its most basic form. More specifically, it discriminates on the basis of gender, race, and geography. One hundred percent diversity infers that some Jewish students from New York City, some Asian students from California, and some white students from Connecticut will not be allowed to attend, even though, based on their past performance in high school, they would probably benefit the most from an Ivy League education. It says to these students that if they want to attend an Ivy League university, they should stop expending their energy in doing better in high school and instead convince their parents to move to Nebraska.

America has fallen in love with diversity. Politicians tell us it is a goal toward which we should all be striving. Even a Supreme Court justice, Powell, said that state universities could strive for diversity when making admissions decisions without violating the Equal Protection Clause of the Fourteenth Amendment. So what's wrong with diversity?

One major problem with it is that, curiously enough, it

assumes sameness and that every institution in America, from the largest corporation to the smallest public school, should have the similar percentages of various races in its workforce. Every agency or government unit should look like every other. No one seems to realize that such sameness could never be achieved absent a massive force, such as a totalitarian government, to enforce it.

Imagine for a moment what America would have to do to achieve the "diversity ideal." First of all, some Asian students would have to be prevented from taking math and science courses in high school and college. There is an overabundance of Asians in the sciences and engineering and not enough of them in other fields. To achieve diversity, they would have to be "made" to be interested in other subjects. There would have to be far fewer Jewish students in law school. African-American and Hispanic students would have to be prevented from going to graduate school in education. There are far too many of them in this field compared with their low representation in other areas. That is the only way America can begin to significantly increase diversity.

What about the public-school faculties? President Clinton has said that he favors 100 percent diversity when it comes to faculties. But he is also 100 percent in support of the racial makeup of the faculty matching that of the student body. The only problem is, he cannot have it both ways. If the faculty reflects the racial composition of the society at large, it is never going to replicate that of the students in any particular school or school district. If we opt for the ideal of racial role models, then we have to abandon the ideal of diversity as well as any attempt to find the very best teachers for students who need the most help, too often poor minority students living in America's urban ghettos. Given the choice between an excellent teacher of the wrong race or a mediocre teacher of the right race, does "diversity" or "role model" mean that another generation of poor minority students will not be prepared for college and the challenges of the modern world? That might have been all right in the old days, when ill-prepared minorities could enter into college and then the job market through the use of racial-preference programs, but those days are coming to an end. In the future, excellence based on education is going to be the only passport to college and a good job. Will strict adherence to diversity or the role-model theory deprive millions of poor minority students of their passport out of the ghetto?

One of the goals of American society, at least according to a number of statutes passed by Congress, is to increase racial integration in America's neighborhoods. What if we actually managed to achieve that goal? What if thousands of white families moved back to Detroit? Given the logic of diversity, there would have to be a racial-preference program to bring more whites into the police and fire departments. In Santa Clara County, California, only 3 percent of the adult working-age population is black, while 6 to 8 percent of the jobs in many of the job categories in county government are held by them. Doesn't diversity demand that Santa Clara County put a freeze on the hiring of blacks in those job categories in which they are overrepresented? If it does not, if we only work toward diversity to the extent that it helps "certain" racial or gender groups, then we are not really working toward diversity, we are engaging in discrimination.

How far is America willing to go to achieve diversity? It is a question no one wants to ask because it is not legitimate to question the accepted wisdom that diversity is just plain good and anyone who doesn't agree must be a racist or a sexist or worst of all, against civil rights. Never mind that the basic theory of civil rights is that everyone in the society should be free to pursue an education and a career without their race or gender being a factor limiting their choices. But if diversity is king, then race and sex will limit their choices. Freedom of choice and total diversity, contrary to the belief of some, are not compatible either in theory or in practice.

In order to achieve gender diversity in the medical profession for the next generation, no women would be admitted to nursing school, and no men would be admitted to medical school. Women are already overrepresented in the nation's law schools when compared to their representation in such occupations as truck driver and loading-dock worker. Are we really prepared, after a century of progress in the area of legal education, to turn women away because of their sex? If we are, then their civil rights, as that concept is generally understood, will be violated. If we are not, then the diversity ideal must suffer.

What would we have to do in order to achieve the totally diverse society? Would we not have to squeeze out the last bit of whatever it is that makes the races and sexes different? Has anyone noticed that to really have total diversity, we would have to forget about the idea of respecting different cultures. You simply cannot have it both ways. Either you respect different cultures and allow some people to pursue careers even where they are overrepresented, or you smash culture and force people to do things they do not want to do.

Voters in California may amend their Constitution to end affirmative-preference programs. What would happen if the voters of California did so? It would mean the end of diversity based on "race, sex, color, ethnicity, or national origin." Would every college campus be mainly Asian and white? No, not necessarily. Colleges would still be free to take poverty into account. That means admissions officers could still consider the life obstacles a student had to overcome to make it through high school when granting admission to college. The poor black, Hispanic, Asian, and white child who grew up without books and a computer in the home could still be granted some kind of special consideration. At the same time, they could not be enrolled without regard to their ability to actually function in college. These poor students would have to provide evidence that they could actually do the work if they had not performed well on the standard admissions test.

What about middle-class minority students? They would have to compete with all the other middle-class students to get into the University of California. If they did not make good grades or do well on the test, they still might be allowed in because of special programs that would still be legal and would give preference to students with a wide variety of special talents, from music to athletics. They would have two bites at the apple: the first, academics; the second, special talent. If they could not do well academically and did not possess any special talent, they would not be able to enter the University of California system. Is that bad? Does it do anyone any good for students who cannot do well academically, who do not have any special talent, and who have not had to overcome personal adversity because of poverty to attend a university?

Let's compare the potential new future to the way it appears to work now. Minority students who would do well in good colleges are admitted to excellent ones where they don't make it. This seems to go on up and down the line of colleges, so that over half of black and Hispanic students who start college never finish. On some campuses in California, such as San Jose State University, the black dropout rate is 75 percent. That is not true at the traditionally black colleges: they take in 15 percent of the black college students every year and turn out 30 percent of all black college graduates. What is it they know that these other colleges don't? Are they successful because they actually try to accept students who can do work at the level required at the particular institution of higher education?

It is important to remember why Justice Powell allowed diversity to rule in the area of college admission. It was not only to help minority students, although that was certainly part of the equation. The stated purpose of diversity on state college campuses was to provide a more diverse educational environment for everyone, minority and nonminority alike. Given an Ivy League setting, the purpose of diversity is to ensure that white students who have never attended a school with blacks or Hispanics can observe them for a while close up before they have to work with them out there in the real world.

Don't talk to a Jewish person about diversity. Geographic diversity was invented as a criteria early in the twentieth century for one reason: to keep Jews out of Ivy League schools. The rationale for this blatant discrimination was that bringing in middle-class students from Iowa and Texas would create some kind of diversity. Upper-middle-class white students from Iowa could then voice opinions that were different from those expressed by upper-middle-class white students from Texas. Stephen Steinberg, writing in *Commentary,* tells us that in 1920, before "diversity," 40 percent of Columbia University's entering students were Jewish. After the "discovery" of geographic diversity, that percentage dropped to 22 percent in two years.[1] He concluded that "the concept of 'regional balance' unquestionably originated as a rationale for discrimination and may well continue as such today."[2] Geographic diversity was a "cover" for anti-Semitic discrimination.

The whole point of diversity on a college campus is exposure to as many points of view as possible. But students are never asked what their point of view is or what ideas they have. Instead, it is assumed, in a very racist way, that if someone is of a different race, he will have a different point of view and different ideas. Does he? That should be an empirical question. After a century of diversity on college campuses, first of the geographic and then of the racial kind, do people from different areas and of different races have fundamentally different points of view? How many of them are communists or fascists or socialists? How many minority students bring anything to campus other than the same middle-class culture that everyone else does?

What would happen if America stopped worshiping diversity as the primary goal in college admissions? What if university admissions committees actually did what Justice Douglas and Justice Powell asked them to do: focused on the individual student seeking admission? What if admissions committees, while making allowances for individual histories, actually tried to determine which students would be most likely to succeed at the particular campus? Of course, it would be more costly than the current system of looking at grades and tests and then "adjusting" to achieve diversity. Just as it is easier for Birmingham, Alabama, to continue to use a race- and gender-biased test and then use a quota to "adjust" in filling city jobs, so, too, it is easier for universities to continue to use grades and tests and then adjust for diversity. But Judge Carnes pointed out in *Ensley Branch, NAACP v. Seibels* (1994) that cities like Birmingham cannot continue such practices if America is ever to get beyond racism and sexism.[3] Isn't the same conclusion inevitable when we examine all the institutions that use diversity as a basis for admissions and promotions? Is not the

152 THE END OF AFFIRMATIVE ACTION

ultimate goal to get beyond quotas and on to a society that treats everyone as an individual?

When Justice Powell's decision in *Bakke* is discussed, it is usually to point out that racial diversity is legal at America's state colleges and universities. What Justice Powell actually said was that a state university's medical school could consider race to be a "plus," along with "exceptional personal talents, unique work or service experience, leadership potential, maturity, demonstrated compassion, a history of overcoming disadvantage, ability to communicate with the poor, and other qualifications deemed important."[4] Justice Powell was not calling for 100 percent racial diversity, and it is doubtful if what generally passes today for diversity would have met with his approval, yet it is what has developed on many university campuses across the country in response to his decision. What would Justice Powell think about the racial quotas that have come to represent the response to the need for diversity?

In northern California, San Jose State and San Francisco State universities are very similar except for the way they treat minority students. San Jose State stresses diversity and is proud of the number of minority students in its entering class. San Francisco State focuses on helping poor minority students in San Francisco prepare to enter and succeed in college. Faculty and students from San Francisco State go out into the community to tutor and advise potential San Francisco State students. These minority students learn early on what they will have to do to succeed in college, and many find that they are perfectly capable of succeeding despite their life histories. San Francisco State places the emphasis on preparing high school students for opportunity rather than on the diversity of its entering class and has a very diverse *graduating* class as a result.

Schools could take another approach when it comes to admissions. Recognizing that it is often not practical to examine every application, they could also acknowledge that admissions tests are not very effective at telling us which students will do better than others. While one who scores very high will probably do better than another who scores very low, there is little evidence that someone who makes a 97 will do better than one who makes a 95. Lani Guinier, a black woman law professor at the University of Pennsylvania, was deemed "too liberal" to be appointed to the Clinton Justice Department. In the January 23, 1995, issue of the *Nation,* she discussed her own ideas concerning how schools could expand opportunity without having to resort to racial quotas or forced diversity.[5] She discussed the "problem" of Lowell High School in San Francisco. Lowell is a magnet school with a national reputation for academic excellence and alumni that include Supreme Court Justice Stephen Breyer. San Francisco public schools are under a court order to ensure racial integration. No one ethnic group may make up more than 40 percent of any magnet school. This has meant that out of a perfect score of 69 on the admissions test, Chinese Americans had to score 66, other Asians and whites had to score 59, and blacks and Hispanics had to score 56. Guinier suggested that San Francisco replace this strict quota system with one that placed the names of everyone scoring over 56 into a hat and selected at random until the entering class was filled. This method would assure some diversity, and it would give everyone who is "capable" of taking full advantage of what Lowell has to offer a chance to enroll without the stigma of racial quotas or the resentment that comes when such tests are assumed to be able to make fine distinctions they really are incapable of making.

This approach could also be used by the University of California. Today the University of California system is supposed to admit the top 12 percent of California's high school graduates. What if the names of the top 20 percent of high school graduates were placed in a hat and pulled out at random. Everyone would be able to do the work and there would be no racial quotas or racial stigma. At the same time, minorities would be admitted to the University of California campuses in substantial numbers. Just as getting away from racial preference in employment will mean using tests to separate those who pass from those who fail and then selecting at random from those who pass, so, too, could the same principle be used by schools when they moved beyond diversity.

There is another problem with the drive to enforce diversity: Ultimately, diversity will come to the extent that America gives everyone the same opportunity to excel. In the year 2000 less than one-third of those entering the workforce in America will be white and male. About a third will be white and female. The rest will be classified as something other than white. We won't have to search for diversity anymore, it will be thrust upon us. It might make more sense if the institutions of America spent more time and money helping to prepare for the time when our workforce will be so diverse. Given such diversity, it is amazing how little the average American really knows about other cultures. Perhaps we could use a few more courses that explain to each of us the basic assumptions of other groups.

Supreme Court Justice Clarence Thomas has now written several decisions concerned with race, education, law, and social policy. While the news media have painted him as some kind of "crazy conservative" and the black establishment has disowned him as some kind of "Uncle Tom," there is much in what he writes that Americans, black and white, would find worth reading. He objects to the supposition that black children can learn only if they are in the presence of white children. In fact, there is no scientific evidence to support it. That was never the real reason America had to integrate her public schools. They had to be integrated because they were segregated, not because black students cannot learn without the presence of white students. In his opinion, the focus should be on equal educational opportunity, not on trying to make sure each class is racially diverse.

There are those who say they are against racial preferences because they amount to discrimination but are in favor of racial diversity. The school board at Pueblo School District No. 60 told that to Connie Cunico when they laid her off because she was white. They were not discriminating against her because of her race; they were simply trying to maintain racial diversity in the workforce.[6] The judges on the Tenth Circuit Court of Appeals did not see the difference. To them it was race discrimination and violated the civil rights laws. Diversity is discrimination.

So what do we do about diversity now? We value it, but we

stop worshiping it. We do so without thinking that every institution must be as diverse as possible or else there is something deeply wrong with it. The twentieth century has taught us that over time groups that were once on the bottom of the economic ladder can move up, given enough opportunity and with the removal of barriers. Irish Catholics, Jews, Chinese, Japanese, Hispanics, and African Americans have all moved up the economic and educational ladder during the century. Given time, opportunity, and a little luck, things change. Irish Catholics are still Catholic, Jews are still Jews, Chinese are still Chinese, Japanese are still Japanese, Hispanics are still Hispanics, and African Americans are still African Americans. It seems reasonable to believe that, over time, more Asian students will major in English literature, and fewer will major in science and math. Government could move mountains to try and speed this process in the name of diversity, but there is little chance that doing so would have much effect.

The focus needs to shift from creating diversity to removing barriers to opportunity. Currently, most Americans live in very segregated neighborhoods. Government has tried, and failed, to force people to live and go to school in more integrated settings. But could government remove barriers to integration? Studies tell us that many minorities are still discriminated against when it comes to being able to borrow money from financial institutions. This is a barrier government can remove. People cannot live where they want to live if they cannot get a mortgage.

Government efforts to remove barriers to opportunity instead of forcing diversity would accomplish more in less time and at a lower social cost. No one thinks that minorities are ever going to achieve the American dream until they receive the same education, financial credit, and employment opportunities that everyone else receives. Creating opportunity is something government can actually foster. Just as America will now have to move from preference to fairness, she must also shift from diversity to opportunity. Opening up opportunities must become the name of the game.

Diversity that flows from greater opportunities will be easy for everyone to accept. The stigma that currently hangs over too many people in too many American institutions will be a thing of the past. Passing out jobs or school admissions to people who have been selected at random from those who "passed" the test will be seen as fair and will still result in racial diversity. It was not fair to assume that these tests can actually distinguish between the best and good enough. They can not. But they can tell us who is reasonably capable of doing the work in both places of employment or in schools. They should be used in a way that makes good use of that information. Students who get into college because they are prepared to succeed instead of because of their race will be more likely to succeed, and their success will be seen by everyone to be deserved. Individual accomplishment will replace quotas, and diversity will still be the result. There is nothing wrong with diversity as a long-term goal of a society committed to creating opportunity for everyone.

11

CONCLUSION

On July 19, 1995, President Clinton gave a speech at the National Archives in which he vowed to fight the Supreme Court's decision in *Adarand*. After that decision America was left with two choices: the country could work to move quickly to the next stage, from affirmative preference to affirmative fairness, or it could spend a decade fighting over the issue, with those supporting preference destined to lose in the end. Apparently, President Clinton has decided to take the second road. As I read about his speech, I could not help but think back to the 1950s and 1960s, when a group of southern white male politicians vowed not to give in to the Supreme Court. They were the governors of states like Alabama, Mississippi, and Arkansas. One literally stood in the schoolhouse door in an effort to stop racial integration of the public schools. Instead of asking how that goal could be achieved with as little pain as possible, they decided to make as much political hay as they could. The result was two decades of social disruption and the abandonment of the inner cities by white people with school-age children. President Clinton has apparently decided to play the race card in 1996. He will probably live to regret that decision. When it comes to the politics of race, the Republicans have won every time.

The Supreme Court ended affirmative-preference programs on June 12, 1995. The headline in the *New York Times* was "Justices Cast New Doubts on Minority Preferences." This headline suggests that someone had "doubts" about what the *Adarand* decision

157

means. There are no doubts. It means that most minority-preference programs are now a part of America's past, not her future.

In the research for their book *The Scar of Race,* Paul Sniderman and Thomas Piazza found that while many whites in America support spending money on social-welfare programs to help the poor, particularly poor blacks, and support the concept of civil rights, they are, and have always been, violently opposed to two programs: busing to achieve racial integration in public schools and affirmative preference based on race. Now, as we approach the end of the twentieth century, both policies are coming to an end, which is something every American, regardless of race or sex, should be glad to see. It means America can move on to the next stage.

Also on June, 12, 1995, the Supreme Court handed down a decision in the case of *Missouri v. Jenkins.*[1] That decision involved what at that point was an eighteen-year-old desegregation lawsuit over the mainly black inner-city schools of Kansas City, Missouri. In that case, the federal district judge ordered the state of Missouri to fund the total rebuilding of the school district and the creation of magnificent magnet schools in an effort to attract white students from the surrounding suburbs. While the physical facilities of the schools are truly magnificent and the black students are certainly taking advantage of them, very few white students have volunteered to attend school in the inner city. The Supreme Court ruled that trying to attract white children from the suburbs was not a legitimate goal of school desegregation. The purpose of a desegregation order is to try to "eliminate the effect of past de jure segregation," not to engage in massive social engineering.

In his concurring decision, Justice Thomas expressed his anger at the idea that black children cannot learn unless they are sitting next to white children. He said: "It never ceases to amaze me that the courts are so willing to assume that anything that is predominantly black must be inferior." He pointed out that the whole idea that black children "suffer an unspecified psychological harm from segregation that retards their mental and educational development" rests on "questionable social science research" and an "assumption of black inferiority," both of which he rejects. He said that segregation was not unconstitutional because it "might have caused psychological feelings of inferiority" for black children but because it violated the principle of equal protection. The whole point of equal protection, in Thomas's opinion, is not to enforce "race mixing" but to ensure that everyone is treated equally.

Justice Thomas makes an important point. The purpose of desegregation was, and still is, to bring an end to a system in which black and white children were kept apart by school district policies. For decades we have equated policies that force black and white children together with desegregation. According to the Supreme Court, however, that is not what desegregation means. Rather, it means making sure that the last vestiges of those "forced segregation" polices are eliminated. In the vast majority of America's public schools we can say with pride that this has been accomplished. It is now possible for America to move past busing to neighborhood schools and magnet schools with special programs. Perhaps some of the whites who moved out of the city to avoid busing may now be tempted to return.

Forced desegregation of inner-city schools in the name of racial integration actually resulted in less integration because of white flight to the suburbs. That the days of busing to achieve racial integration are coming to an end should be cause for celebration by both blacks and whites alike. Parents, both black and white, are generally in favor of their children attending the neighborhood school, not taking long bus rides to somewhere else. In cities across America, magnet schools are succeeding in bringing the races together in situations where everyone attends that particular school because they want to, not because they were forced to by federal court order. It has taken half a century, but America's schools are making progress when it comes to racial integration.

Too many leaders, black and white, have been slow to realize the potential advantages that can flow from the changes that are already here. For several decades America has struggled to end the vestiges of legal school segregation through busing and to jump-start integration through affirmative-preference programs. Both policies were necessary but costly. They led to more racial tension, not less. Sniderman and Piazza's finding that the "mere mention" of affirmative preference in a "nearby state" increased feelings of antagonism by whites against blacks confirms what many people already thought: that these policies, while necessary, were increasing the racial divide in America, not diminishing it.[2]

Throughout the decades of forced busing and affirmative preference, a large majority of whites were against both policies. What often went unreported was that a substantial percentage of minorities also opposed them. Americans have been strangely united in opposition to policies which the judges and politicians felt were necessary but the general public found to be difficult to accept. Now these policies are coming to an end. Some leaders seem to think that this is a dark day for race relations in America. On the contrary, it should be cause for celebration. But there are still massive problems to be overcome.

In the 1950s, 50 percent of African-American women who worked were domestic servants. By the 1990s that percentage had dropped to less than 3 percent. While we might be tempted to see this as progress, that statistic hides what is in reality two phenomena. For many black women who were able to graduate from high school, or better yet, college, the fact that they counted twice under the affirmative-preference system, once as minorities and once as women, gave them tremendous opportunities. These women no longer needed to consider working as domestic servants. Statistics tell us that there are now more black women with MBA, law, engineering, and accounting degrees than black men. What about the African-American women who did not graduate from high school and might have been willing to work as domestic servants? They found that the jobs had been taken by new immigrants from Asia and Latin America, many of them illegal and willing to work for illegally low wages. For these black women the statistic simply reflects the fact that for them even a job as a domestic servant has been foreclosed. Their fate is not a cause for celebration.

Affirmative preference has helped African Americans and

other minorities who managed to get an education. The "new" black middle class is real and growing and has benefited from affirmative preference. But this should not be allowed to mask the fact that one-third of African Americans live in poverty, many in inner cities where drugs, crime, unemployment, hopelessness, and despair are everyday facts of life. All the affirmative-preference programs in the world are not going to make any difference in their lives. This is where Sniderman and Piazza's research offers hope. They found that white Americans recognize the problem and are willing to spend money to correct it.

During the twentieth century the United States has spent $5 trillion on nuclear weapons alone. Now it needs to spend 1 percent of that amount a year for a decade to rebuild the fifty worst inner-city urban slums. A billion dollars a year spent in each would make a difference, and in each, a federal "reconstruction czar" would be in charge of the money. He or she would have five firm goals: first, to increase the level of home ownership; second, to increase the level of high school graduation; third, to raise the level of employment; fourth, to decrease the level of street crime; and fifth, to improve the general attractiveness of the area. The economic reality is that many of America's worst slums are a few subway stops away from the most expensive real estate in the country. Harlem is now synonymous with the word slum, but it was once a showcase of new apartment buildings and innovative public services. The eastern half of Washington, D.C., could be a showcase to the world of how to renovate an inner city. The major obstacle to change in these and other cities is the lack of money. Money cannot solve every problem, but it can help people buy a home, stay in school, renovate a park, attract an employer, and pay police for overtime. Where would we get the money? America currently spends $150 billion a year on corporate welfare in the form of tax breaks and outright subsidies. Why not reduce corporate welfare by one-third and use the money to rebuild the inner cities?

While there are those who might argue that Americans are not willing to spend the money, survey research suggests otherwise. Even conservative Americans recognize that for many black people who live in the inner city the legacy of racism is still a very big factor in their lives. Most Americans also realize that crack cocaine is not a part of everyday life in the suburbs, but it is in many inner cities. When white families fled to the suburbs, the inner cities lost jobs, while the suburbs gained jobs, particularly the kinds that require less education. Ways need to be found to make it easier for low-skill workers to get to where the low-skill jobs are. If the new "reconstruction czars" were given the power to fund free day care for every child in the urban slums—safe, competent, efficient day care—it would mean a major step forward in the lives of everyone.

On July 20, 1995, Jesse Jackson gave a speech before the University of California Board of Regents in an effort to convince them not to end affirmative-preference programs based on race. He told them about growing up in the South, about the lack of "black only" public rest rooms, and about the humiliation he felt as a young black man. But that is all history, and every American can be proud of the fact that we have come so far. Jesse Jackson needs to stop looking back and to start looking forward. Not all African Americans feel the way he does. A few months before Jesse Jackson made his speech, Lani Guinier made one at the National Press Club in which she argued that America must get "beyond the notion that racial preferences are the only or best way to remedy racial inequality."[3]

While the citizens of California have made it clear that they are no longer willing to suffer racial-preference programs, that is not necessarily bad for black Americans. Many forget that when Allan Bakke sued the University of California Medical School at Davis, only a third of the "special admissions" had gone to black people. While some estimate that during the 1970s from one-half to one-third of the "benefit" of affirmative preference went to blacks, no one believes it amounts to more than a fourth in the 1990s. We might well ask if it makes sense for African-American leaders to expend so much of their political capital on a program that now mainly helps people other than African Americans. While African Americans receive less and less concrete benefit from affirmative preference, they are still more stigmatized by it. Most of the students admitted under the special-admissions program at the University of California Medical School at Davis were Asian and Hispanic. Yet when Americans look at an Asian or Hispanic doctor, they do not see a big "A" on his or her forehead for affirmative action. That honor is reserved for African-American doctors.

While the University of California removes special-admissions programs based on race, it can introduce them based on poverty. There are still plenty of poor African Americans in California who could benefit from such a change. Some might argue that poverty-based programs would have a greater impact on African Americans than race-based programs. We know from research done at the University of Maryland that many of the minorities who drop out of large public universities do so not because of their race but because of poverty. It is the need to work full-time and live far from campus that drives them out of college, not the inability to do the work. All the affirmative preference programs in the world are not going to do anything about that problem; spending more money would actually help.

America needs to come face-to-face with the fact that most of the tests she uses to make millions of selection decisions are currently being misused. They simply are not capable of making the fine distinctions that they are being called upon to make. A score of 77 is not really better than a score of 75 on a test with a margin of error of two points. While employment and school-admissions tests could be used to separate out the highly qualified from the qualified and the unqualified, that is all they could do. The highly qualified should get the job or the place in school regardless of the person's race or sex. To the extent that there are more jobs or places, the names of the qualified should be put into a hat and drawn out at random until the jobs or places have been filled. There is good reason to believe that this procedure will result in just about as much race and gender diversity as the current "quota" system—and without the stigma.

When Shelby Steele says that affirmative-preference programs have been "too easy" and that we must now get on with the hard part, he is absolutely right. We will have to make sure that hiring and promotion decisions are made fairly, without gender or racial bias, and that will not be easy. We will have to work to ensure that all children in America receive a quality education regardless of their parent's wealth or social standing. We will have to rebuild America's inner cities.

But in many ways these policies should be easier because everyone, regardless of race, believes in them, at least according to survey research. Congress will no longer need to pass "stealth statutes" or hide its support for these programs inside appropriations bills. Presidents will actually be able to support such programs without saying one thing and doing another.

Democracy, liberty, political equality, and equal opportunity—these are the four cornerstones of American society. For too long Americans have had to endure policies which ignored one or more of these principles in the name of being able to better achieve them "someday." Someday is here.

When I read about African-American businesspeople moving to South Africa to launch businesses that will help develop that economy, I am proud to be an American. When a friend moves to Chili to teach how to turn workers into stockholders, I can only wish him well. When the Vietnamese student I helped tutor for the law-school entrance exam says she wants to work to help Vietnam understand how law works in a free society, I can only say, "God speed." While these are all reasons to hope, there is still much to regret. When I walk into a hamburger joint in Oakland and find a young black woman speaking perfect English to me and fluent Spanish to the cook, I am angry. She should be working in an American corporation helping to ensure our economic future, not waiting tables. When I see a bright black student settle for a master's degree in "educational administration" because the federal government will give him financial help if he does so, I am angry. He should be able to be anything he wants to be, from nuclear physicist to president of a major corporation. The federal government should not have foreclosed his choices in life.

For too long Americans have been willing to settle for symbolic answers to real problems. When Congress decided to do something about illegal aliens, it passed a law that required every employer to fill out a form each time they hired someone. This resulted in a new business for organized crime: printing up fake identification cards. It did not reduce illegal immigration. When Congress decided to do something about assault weapons, it passed a law that resulted in the slight modification of a few weapons. It did not reduce the sale of assault weapons. These and many other federal statutes are simply symbolic. During the first hundred days of the 1995 session, Congress did not repeal one law or eliminate one federal agency. Despite all the talk, everything is still the same.

What about the law of equal protection? It is currently being written by the first woman and the second African American to ever sit on the U.S. Supreme Court. They are demanding that equal protection mean just that—for everyone—and that we move away from policies which assume that minorities and women cannot compete simply because of their race or sex. They recognize the arguments that have been made for a transition period based on affirmative preference, but they no longer believe it is necessary. In their opinion, if affirmative preference and federal control of local schools were necessary to move America to the next stage, then it is time to move into that next stage.

Justice Blackmun hoped that the time would come when America could move from race consciousness to race blindness. Justice Powell emphasized the need to create "temporary" programs to deal with past injustice. Justice Brennan emphasized that regardless of how students enter a university, they are entitled to the same education that other students get. Justice Douglas believed that every student deserves a fair chance to succeed regardless of his or her economic circumstances. Justice Marshall argued eloquently for an end to laws based on race. All these justices spoke in favor of some kind of temporary period of affirmative preference.

None of the justices provided us with any kind of yardstick to measure when it is time to end affirmative preference. When will we be able to say that we are ready to move as a society beyond preference to fairness? There will never be a time when everyone can agree that the time has come. It was the justices of the

Supreme Court who decided that the affirmative-preference period could begin. It is the justices of the Supreme Court who have decided that it must now end. Perhaps we should have continued on for another decade, but that is no longer an option. What has been lost in much of the rhetoric of 1995 is the simple fact that affirmative preference is a thing of the past. The Supreme Court brought it to an end on June 12, 1995. It is time for everyone to understand what that means.

Affirmative preference is a part of America's past, not her future. The future will have to concentrate on finding the true meaning of the phrase "equal protection of the laws." Giving real meaning to this phrase has been a long and difficult task, and it is not over, but phase one is. America is moving into phase two. Making the new phase a success will require the goodwill of every American regardless of race or sex. It will require recognizing the lingering impact of past sexism and racism. It will require spending money to bring a lost segment of society in the inner cities of America up to the starting line. It will require bending over backwards to assure that decisions are made fairly and without bias. It will not be easy.

But the rewards could be truly amazing. At last, the greatest nation on earth will be united as never before and dedicated to living out her creed. As Martin Luther King Jr. said, it is a creed all Americans can be proud of. It is a creed based on one statement: "We hold these truths to be self-evident; that all men are created equal." King had a dream that one day he would see a nation truly live out the full meaning of that creed. That day is closer than when he spoke on August 28, 1963, about his dream for America. He dreamed of a day:

> when all of God's children will be able to sing with new meaning, "My country 'tis of thee, sweet land of liberty of thee I sing. Land where my fathers died, land of the Pilgrims' pride, from every mountainside, let freedom ring....
>
> When we let freedom ring, when we let it ring from every village and hamlet, from every state and every city,

we will be able to speed up the day when all of God's children, black men and white men, Jews and Gentiles, Protestants and Catholics, will be able to join hands and sing in the words of the old Negro spiritual: "Free at last! Free at last! Thank God Almighty, we are free at last."

We can all be proud of the fact that we are closer to that day. We can all dedicate ourselves to taking the next step of a very long journey. It is a journey America had to take, and the end is in sight. It is a journey from slavery to freedom, from inequality to equality, from injustice to justice. The last leg of the journey will be difficult but not impossible. It is a parade we can all march in.

When Thomas Jefferson wrote the words that begin the Declaration of Independence, he knew that all men were not equal and it would be a long time before they would be. The problem of race in America was one for which he had no answer. The answer has been long in coming. In the final analysis, the path to equality must be equality. There really is no other way.

APPENDIX

TABLE OF CASES

Price Waterhouse v. Hopkins, 490 U.S. 228 (1989).
Regents of the University of California v. Bakke, 438 U.S. 265 (1978).
Rostker v. Goldberg, 453 U.S. 464 (1981).
Sheet Metal Workers v. EEOC, 478 U.S. 421 (1986).
Steelworkers v. Weber, 443 U.S. 193 (1979).
Strauder v. West Virginia, 100 U.S. 303 (1879).
Sweatt v. Painter, 339 U.S. 629 (1950).
United States v. Paradise, 480 U.S. 149 (1987).
Wards Cove Packing Co. v. Atonio, 490 U.S. 642 (1989).
Wygant v. Jackson Board of Education, 476 U.S. 267 (1986).
Yick Wo v. Hopkins, 118 U.S. 356 (1886).

CIRCUIT COURT

Associated General Contractors v. City of San Francisco, 813 F. 2d 922 (9th Cir. 1987).
Bishopp v. District of Columbia, 788 F. 2d 781 (D.C. Cir. 1986).
Contractors Association v. Philadelphia, 6 F. 3d 990 (3d Cir. 1993).
Coral Construction v. King County, 941 F. 2d 910 (9th Cir. 1991).
Cunico v. Pueblo School District No. 60, 917 F. 2d 431 (10th Cir. 1990).
Detroit Police Officer's Association v. Young, 989 F. 2d 225 (6th Cir. 1993).
Edwards v. City of Houston, 37 F. 3d 1097 (5th Cir. 1994).
Ensley Branch, NAACP v. Seibels, 31 F. 3d 1548 (11th Cir. 1994).
Harrison & Burrowes v. Cuomo, 981 F. 2d 50 (2d Cir. 1992).
Hopwood v. University of Texas School of Law, not yet reported.
Jett v. Dallas ISD, 798 F. 2d 748 (5th Cir. 1986).
Long v. City of Saginaw, 911 F. 2d 1192 (6th Cir. 1990).
Maryland Troopers Association v. Evans, 993 F. 2d 1072 (4th Cir. 1993).
Milwaukee County Pavers v. Fiedler, 922 F. 2d 419 (7th Cir. 1991).
O'Donnell Construction v. District of Columbia, 963 F. 2d 420 (D.C. Cir. 1992).
Peightal v. Dade County, 26 F. 3d 1545 (11th Cir. 1994).
Podberesky v. Kirwan, 38 F. 3d 147 (4th Cir. 1994).
Taxman v. Board of Education of Piscataway, not yet reported.
Tennessee Asphalt v. Ferris, 942 F. 2d 969 (6th Cir. 1991).
United Black Firefighter's Association v. Akron, 976 F. 2d 999 (6th Cir. 1992).
Walters v. City of Atlanta, 803 F. 2d 1135 (11th Cir. 1986).

NOTES

CHAPTER 1

1. Richard Morin. "No Place for Calm and Quiet Opinions," *Washington Post* 12, no. 25 (April 24–30, 1995), 34, National Weekly edition.

CHAPTER 2

1. Dred Scott v. Sandford, 60 U.S. 393 (1857).
2. Civil Rights Cases, 109 U.S. 3 (1883).
3. Title 42 of the U.S. Code, Sections 1981, 1982, 1983, 1985; Title 18 of the U.S. Code, Sections 241, 242.
4. Plessy v. Ferguson, 163 U.S. 537 (1896).
5. Missouri v. Canada, 305 U.S. 337 (1938).
6. Sweatt v. Painter, 339 U.S. 629 (1950).
7. Brown v. Board of Education, 347 U.S. 483 (1954); Brown v. Board of Education II, 349 U.S. 294 (1955).
8. Title 42 of the U.S. Code, Section 2000e.
9. Title 42 of the U.S. Code, Section 1973.
10. Jones v. Alfred H. Mayer Co., 392 U.S. 409 (1968).
11. Price Waterhouse v. Hopkins, 490 U.S. 228 (1989); Wards Cove Packing Co. v. Atonio, 490 U.S. 642 (1989); Martin v. Wilkes, 490 U.S. 755 (1989); Lorance v. AT&T, 490 U.S. 900 (1989); Patterson v. McLean Credit Union, 491 U.S. 164 (1989).
12. Miller v. Johnson, 115 S. Ct. 2475 (1995).

CHAPTER 3

1. Earl Raab, "Quotas by Any Other Name," *Commentary,* January 1972, 41–45.
2. Paul Seaburg, "HEW and the Universities," *Commentary,* February 1972, 38–44.

3. Elliott Abrams, "Quota Commission," *Commentary,* October 1972, 54–57.

4. Regents of the University of California v. Bakke, 438 U.S. 265 (1978); Steelworkers v. Weber, 443 U.S. 193 (1979); Fullilove v. Klutznick, 448 U.S. 448 (1980).

5. Daniel Seligman, "Affirmative Action is Here to Stay," *Fortune,* April 19, 1982, 143–162.

6. Anne Fisher, "Businessmen Like to Hire by the Numbers," *Fortune,* September 16, 1985, 26–30.

CHAPTER 4

1. John Harris and Kevin Merida, "Affirmative Action Under Fire," *Washington Post,* 12, no. 25 (April 24–30, 1995), 6–7, National Weekly edition.

2. Alan Farnham, "Holding Firm on Affirmative Action," *Fortune,* March 13, 1989, 87–88.

3. Walters v. City of Atlanta, 803 F. 2d 1135 (11th Cir. 1986).

4. Jett v. Dallas ISD, 798 F. 2d 748 (5th Cir. 1986).

5. Bishopp v. District of Columbia, 788 F. 2d 781 (D.C. Cir. 1986).

6. Peter Brimelow and Leslie Spencer, "When Quotas Replace Merit, Everybody Suffers," *Forbes,* February 15, 1993, 82, 80–102.

7. Robert Weissberg, "The Gypsy Scholars," *Forbes,* May 10, 1993, 138.

CHAPTER 5

1. John Leo, "Endgame for Affirmative Action," *U.S. News & World Report,* March 13, 1995, p. 18.

2. Thomas Sowell, "Are Quotas Good for Blacks?" *Commentary,* June 1978, 39–43.

3. _____. *Ethnic America* (New York: Basic Books, 1981).

4. _____. "Busing and Affirmative Action, Neither Do Much Good," *New York Times Magazine,* August 8, 1976, 14–45.

5. Bron Taylor, *Affirmative Action at Work* (Pittsburg: University of Pittsburg Press, 1991).

6. Marsha Jacobson and Walter Kich, "Women as Leaders: Performance Evaluation as a Function of Method of Leader Selection," *Organizational Behavior and Human Performance* 20 (1977), 149–57.

7. Thomas Chacko, "Women and Equal Employment Opportunity:

Some Unintended Efffects," *Journal of Applied Psychology* 67, no. 1, (1982), 119–23.

8. Madeline Heilman and Joyce Herlihy, "Affirmative Action Negative Reaction? Some Moderating Conditions," *Organizational Behavior and Human Performance,* 33, (1984), 204–13.

9. Madeline Heilman, Michael Simon, and David Repper, "Intentionally Favored, Unintentionally Harmed: Impact of Sex-Based Preferential Selection on Self-Perception and Self-Evaluation," *Journal of Applied Psychology* 72, (1987), 62–68.

10. Madeline Heilman, Jonathan Lucas, and Stella Kaplow, "Self-Derogating Consequences of Sex-Based Preferential Selection: the Moderating Role of Initial Self-Confidence," *Organizational Behavior and Human Decision Processes* 46 (1990), 202–16.

11. Madeline Heilman, Carlos Rivera, and Joan Bratt, "Skirting the Competence Issue: Effects of Sex-Based Preferential Selection on Task Choices of Women and Men," *Journal of Applied Psychology* 76, (1991), 99–105.

12. Rupert Nacoste, "Affirmative Action and Self-Evaluation," in *Affirmative Action in Perspective,* eds. F. A. Blancard and F. J. Crosby (New York: Springer-Verlag, 1989).

13. Paul Sniderman and Thomas Piazza, *The Scar of Race* (Cambridge, Mass.: Harvard University Press, 1993).

CHAPTER 6

1. Dred Scott v. Sandford, 60 U.S. 393 (1857).
2. Plessy v. Ferguson, 163 U.S. 537 (1896).
3. Strauder v. West Virginia, 100 U.S. 303 (1879).
4. Yick Wo v. Hopkins, 118 U.S. 356 (1886).
5. Korematsu v. United States, 323 U.S. 214 (1944).
6. Brown v. Board of Education, 347 U.S. 483 (1954).
7. Milliken v. Bradley, 418 U.S. 717 (1974).
8. Adkins v. Children's Hospital, 261 U.S. 525 (1923).
9. Goesaert v. Cleary, 335 U.S. 464 (1948).
10. Frontiero v. Richardson, 411 U.S. 677 (1973).
11. Craig v. Boren, 429 U.S. 190 (1976).
12. Califano v. Webster, 430 U.S. 313 (1977).
13. Mississippi Women's University v. Hogan, 458 U.S. 718 (1982).
14. Rostker v. Goldberg, 453 U.S. 464 (1981).
15. DeFunis v. Odegaard, 416 U.S. 312 (1974).

CHAPTER 7

1. Regents of the University of California v. Bakke, 438 U.S. 265 (1978).

2. Steelworkers v. Weber, 443 U.S. 193 (1979).

3. Fullilove v. Klutznick, 448 U.S. 448 (1980).

4. Firefighters v. Stotts, 467 U.S. 561 (1984).

5. Wygant v. Jackson Board of Education, 476 U.S. 267 (1986).

6. Sheet Metal Workers v. EEOC, 478 U.S. 421 (1986).

7. United States v. Paradise, 480 U.S. 149 (1987).

8. Johnson v. Santa Clara County, 480 U.S. 1442 (1987).

9. City of Richmond v. Croson, 488 U.S. 469 (1989).

10. Metro Broadcasting Inc. v. FCC, 497 U.S. 547 (1990).

11. Adarand Constructors v. Pena, 115 S. Ct. 2097 (1995).

12. Taxman v. Board of Education of Piscataway, not yet reported.

13. William Kilberg, "Affirmative Action: the Clinton Administration Weighs in," *Employee Relations Law Journal* 20 (Spring 1995), 499–501.

CHAPTER 8

1. Donovan Bigelow, "Equal but Separate: Can the Army's Affirmative Action Program Withstand Judicial Scrutiny After *Croson?*" *Military Law Review,* 131 (1991) 147.

2. Coral Construction v. King County, 941 F. 2d 910 (9th Cir. 1991).

3. Milwaukee County Pavers v. Fiedler, 922 F. 2d 419 (7th Cir. 1991).

4. O'Donnell Construction v. District of Columbia, 963 F. 2d 420 (D.C. Cir. 1992).

5. Contractors Association v. Philadelphia, 6 F. 3d 990 (3d Cir. 1993).

6. Tennessee Asphalt v. Ferris, 942 F. 2d 969 (6th Cir. 1991).

7. Harrison & Burrowes v. Cuomo, 981 F. 2d 50 (2d Cir. 1992).

8. Long v. City of Saginaw, 911 F. 2d 1192 (6th Cir. 1990).

9. United Black Firefighter's Association v. Akron, 976 F. 2d 999 (6th Cir. 1992).

10. Detroit Police Officer's Association v. Young, 989 F. 2d 225 (6th Cir. 1993).

11. Maryland Troopers Association v. Evans, 993 F. 2d 1072 (4th Cir. 1993).

12. Cunico v. Pueblo School District No. 60, 917 F. 2d 431 (10th Cir. 1990).

13. Peightal v. Dade County, 26 F. 3d 1545 (11th Cir. 1994).

14. Edwards v. City of Houston, 37 F. 3d 1097 (5th Cir. 1994).

15. Associated General Contractors v. City of San Francisco, 813 F. 2d 922 (9th Cir. 1987).

16. Podberesky v. Kirwan, 38 F. 3d 147 (4th Cir. 1994).

17. Hopwood v. University of Texas School of Law, not yet reported.

18. Sweatt v. Painter, 339 U.S. 629 (1950).

19. Ensley Branch, NAACP v. Seibels, 31 F. 3d 1548 (11th Cir. 1994).

20. Steelworkers v. Weber, 443 U.S. 193 (1979), and Johnson v. Santa Clara County, 480 U.S. 1442 (1987).

CHAPTER 9

1. Steven L. Carter, *Reflections of an Affirmative Action Baby* (New York: Basic Books, 1991).

2. Plessy v. Ferguson, 163 U.S. 537 (1896).

3. Plessy v. Ferguson, 163 U.S. 537 (1896); Dred Scott v. Sandford, 60 U.S. 393 (1857).

4. Study cited in Podberesky v. Kirwan, 38 F. 3d 147 (4th Cir. 1994).

5. Katha Pollitt, "Subject to Debate," *The Nation*, March 13, 1995, 336.

6. Metro Broadcasting v. FCC, 497 U.S. 547 (1990).

7. Executive Orders 10925, 11246.

8. Adarand Constructors v. Pena, 115 S. Ct. 2097 (1995).

9. Johnson v. Santa Clara County, 480 U.S. 1442 (1987).

10. Dale Russakoff, "Struggling with the Stigma of a Special Status," *Washington Post*. 12, no. 25 (April 24–30, 1995), 8–9, National Weekly edition.

CHAPTER 10

1. Stephen Steinberg, "How Jewish Quotas Began," *Commentary*, September 1971, 67–76.

2. Ibid., 76.

3. Ensley Branch, NAACP v. Seibels, 31 F. 3d 1548 (11th Cir. 1994).

4. Regents of the University of California v. Bakke, 438 U.S. 265 (1978).

5. Lani Guinier, "Democracy's Conversation," *The Nation*, January 23, 1995, 85–88.

6. Cunico v. Pueblo School District No. 60, 917 F. 2d 431 (10th Cir. 1990).

CHAPTER 11

1. Missouri v. Jenkins, 115 S. Ct. 2038 (1995).

2. Paul Sniderman and Thomas Piazza, *The Scar of Race* (Cambridge, Mass.: Harvard University Press, 1993).

3. Lani Guinier, "Democracy's Conversation," *The Nation*, January 23, 1995, 86.

SELECT BIBLIOGRAPHY

Abrams, Elliot. "Quota Commission," *Commentary*, October 1972, 54–57.

Adelson, Joseph. "Living With Quotas," *Commentary*, May 1978, 23–29.

Altschiller, Donald, ed. *Affirmative Action*. New York: H. W. Wilson Co., 1991.

Bennett, William, and Terry Eastland. "Why Bakke Won't End Reverse Discrimination," *Commentary*, September 1978, 29–35.

————. *Counting by Race*. New York: Basic Books, 1979.

Bernstein, Peter. "Quotas Live On," *Fortune*, July 23, 1984, 95–96.

Bigelow, Donovan. "Equal but Separate: Can the Army's Affirmative Action Program Withstand Judicial Scrutiny After *Croson*?" *Military Law Review*, 131 (1991), 147.

Blanchard, F. A., and F. J. Crosby, eds. *Affirmative Action in Perspective*. New York: Springer-Verlag, 1989.

Bowie, Norman, ed. *Equal Opportunity*. Boulder, Colo.: Westview Press, 1988.

Brimelow, Peter, and Leslie Spencer. "When Quotas Replace Merit, Everybody Suffers," *Forbes*, February 15, 1993, 82, 80–102.

Brooks, Roy. *Rethinking the American Race Problem*. Berkeley, Calif.: University of California Press, 1990.

Carter, Steven L. *Reflections of an Affirmative Action Baby*. New York: Basic Books, 1991.

Chacko, Thomas. "Women and Equal Employment Opportunity: Some Unintended Effects," *Journal of Applied Psychology* 67, no. 1, (1982), 119–23.

Cohen, Carl. "Justice Debased: The Weber Decision," *Commentary*, September 1979, 43–53.

————. "Why Racial Preference Is Illegal and Immoral," *Commentary*, June 1979, 40–52.

Combs, Michael, and John Gruhl, eds. *Affirmative Action: Theory, Analysis and Prospects*. Jefferson, N.C.: McFarland & Co., 1986.

Coss, Ellias. *The Rage of a Privileged Class.* New York: HarperCollins, 1993.

Epstein, Richard. *Forbidden Grounds: The Case Against Discrimination Laws.* Cambridge, Mass.: Harvard University Press, 1992.

Farnham, Alan. "Holding Firm on Affirmative Action," *Fortune,* March 13, 1989, 87–88.

Fine, Chester. "Affirmative Action Under Reagan," *Commentary,* April 1982, 17–28.

————. "Quotas and the Bush Administration," *Commentary,* November 1991, 17–23.

Fisher, Anne. "Businessmen Like to Hire by the Numbers," *Fortune,* September 16, 1985, 26–30.

Fried, Charles. "Affirmative Action After *City of Richmond v. Croson:* A Response to the Scholar's Statement" *Yale Law Journal,* 99, (1989), 155.

Glazer, Nathan. *Affirmative Discrimination: Ethnic Inequality and Public Policy.* New York: Basic Books, 1975.

Glendon, Mary. *Rights Talk: The Impoverishment of Political Discourse.* New York: Free Press, 1993.

Greene, Kathanne. *Affirmative Action and Principles of Justice.* Westport, Conn.: Greenwood Press, 1989.

Guinier, Lani. "Democracy's Conversation," *The Nation,* January 23, 1995, 85–88.

Harris, John, and Kevin Merida. "Affirmative Action Under Fire," *Washington Post,* 12, no. 25, (April 24–30, 1995), 6–7. National Weekly edition.

Heilman, Madeline, and Joyce Herlihy. "Affirmative Action Negative Reaction? Some Moderating Conditions," *Organizational Behavior and Human Performance,* 33 (1984), 204–13.

Heilman, Madeline, Michael Simon, and David Repper. "Intentionally Favored, Unintentionally Harmed: Impact of Sex-Based Preferential Selection on Self-Perception and Self-Evaluation," *Journal of Applied Psychology* 72 (1987), 62–68.

Heilman, Madeline, Jonathan Lucas, and Stella Kaplow. "Self-Derogating Consequences of Sex-Based Preferential Selection: the Moderating Role of Initial Self-Confidence," *Organizational Behavior and Human Decision Processes,* 46 (1990), 202–16.

Heilman, Madeline, Carlos Rivera, and Joan Bratt. "Skirting the Competence Issue: Effects of Sex-Based Preferential Selection on Task

Choices of Women and Men," *Journal of Applied Psychology* 76, (1991), 99–105.

Hoffman, Lori. "Fatal in Fact: An Analysis of the Application of the Compelling Governmental Interest Leg of Strict Scrutiny in *City of Richmond v. Croson*," *Boston University Law Review* 70 (1990), 889.

Horne, Gerald. *Reverse Discrimination: The Case for Affirmative Action*. New York: International Publishers, 1992.

Jacobson, Marsha, and Walter Kich. "Women as Leaders: Performance Evaluation as a Function of Method of Leader Selection," *Organizational Behavior and Human Performance* 20 (1977), 149–57.

Kilberg, William. "Affirmative Action: the Clinton Administration Weighs In," *Employee Relations Law Journal* 20 (Spring 1995), 499–501.

Kristol, Irving. "How Hiring Quotas Came to Campus," *Fortune*, 90 no. 3 (September 1974), 203–7.

Leo, John. "Endgame for Affirmative Action," *U.S. News & World Report*, March 13, 1995, 18.

———. "Feel Abused? Get in Line," *U.S. News & World Report*, April 10, 1995, 21.

Lynch, Frederick. "Surviving Affirmative Action (More or Less)," *Commentary*, August 1990, 44–47.

McWhirter, Darien. *Your Rights At Work*, 2d ed. New York: Wiley, 1993.

———. *Equal Protection*. Phoenix, Ariz.: Oryx Press, 1995.

Mead, Lawence. *The New Politics of Poverty*. New York: Basic Books, 1992.

Mills, Nicolaus, ed. *Debating Affirmative Action*. New York: Delta Publishing, 1994.

Morin, Richard. "No Place for Calm and Quiet Opinions," *Washington Post*, 12, no. 25 (April 24–30, 1995), 34. National Weekly edition.

Nacoste, Rupert. "Affirmative Action and Self-Evaluation," in *Affirmative Action in Perspective*, eds. by F. A. Blancard and F. J. Crosby. New York: Springer-Verlag, 1989.

Pollitt, Katha, "Subject to Debate," *The Nation*, March 13, 1995, 336.

Raab, Earl. "Quotas by Any Other Name," *Commentary*, January 1972, 41–45.

Rosenfeld, Michel. *Affirmative Action and Justice*. New Haven, Conn.: Yale University Press, 1991.

Russakoff, Dale. "Struggling with the Stigma of a Special Status," *Washington Post*. 12, no. 25 (April 24–30, 1995), 8–9. National Weekly edition.

Schlesinger, Arthur. *The Disuniting of America*. Knoxville, Tenn.: Whittle Communications, 1991.

Schwarz, Jordan. *The New Dealers: Power Politics in the Age of Roosevelt*. New York: Alfred A. Knopf, 1993.

Seaburg, Paul. "HEW and the Universities," *Commentary*, February 1972, 38–44.

Seligman, Daniel. "Affirmative Action Is Here to Stay," *Fortune*, April 19, 1982, 143–162.

———. "Johnson v. Santa Clara County," *Fortune*, April 27, 1987, 283–86.

———. "Quotas on Campus," *Fortune*, January 30, 1989, 205–8.

Sniderman, Paul, and Thomas Piazza. *The Scar of Race*. Cambridge, Mass.: Harvard University Press, 1993.

Sowell, Thomas. "Busing and Affirmative Action, Neither Do Much Good," *New York Times Magazine*, August 8, 1976, 14–45.

———. "Are Quotas Good for Blacks?" *Commentary*, June 1978, 39–43.

———. *Ethnic America*. New York: Basic Books, 1981.

Steele, Shelby. *The Content of Our Character*. New York: St. Martin's Press, 1990.

Steinberg, Stephen. "How Jewish Quotas Began," *Commentary*, September 1971, 67–76.

Sykes, Charles. *A Nation of Victims*. New York: St. Martin's Press, 1992.

Taylor, Bron. *Affirmative Action at Work*. Pittsburg: University of Pittsburg Press, 1991.

Turner, Ronald. *The Past and Future of Affirmative Action*. New York: Quorum Books, 1990.

Weissberg, Robert. "The Gypsy Scholars," *Forbes*, May 10, 1993, 138.

Yates, Steven. *Civil Wrongs: What Went Wrong With Affirmative Action*. San Francisco, Calif.: Institute for Contemporary Studies, 1994.

Zuckerman, Mortimer. "Fixing Affirmative Action," *U.S. News & World Report*, March 20, 1995, 112.

INDEX